WALKING ON ICE

Emma Stevens

This memoir is based on fact, however, some names have been changed to protect the identity of individuals.

Published 2014
by Emma Stevens
www.walkingonice.co.nz

ISBN 978-0-473-30617-5

© Copyright 2014
All rights reserved.

Except for the purpose of fair reviewing, no part of this publication may be reproduced or transmitted in any form or by any means, electronic or mechanical, including photocopying, recording or any information storage and retrieval system, without prior written permission from the publisher.

Printed by The Copy Press, Nelson, New Zealand. www.copypress.co.nz

To My Mother

*'Come and sit with me dear,
and tell me all about your day'*

Chapter 1

Bound for Bush Alaska

Flying up and out across the western Alaskan mountain range I could see the city of Anchorage gradually shrinking from view. Towering peaks of snow-covered ridges stood sentry to the vast landscapes that lay beyond. The small Beechcraft 1900, with its eight bush-bound passengers, hummed bravely into the chill wind of late autumn. The remoteness that lay beyond these ranges was stunning, dramatic and so vast I felt scared. I needed time to relax. Soon I would be there. I had left Christchurch airport, in the South Island of New Zealand, on a journey that had taken me across the world.

One day earlier, en route, I had found myself under police escort at LA airport. It was nearly two weeks after 9/11, and a bomb scare at the airport while I was awaiting my Alaskan flight had everyone skittish. I had moved away from the crowd, the people who had all dutifully lined up in the restricted area following the scare announcement, because I needed to call Gary and warn him of this potential delay.

My move over to the payphones had alerted the LA ground police. My dark red hair, black clothing and Maori greenstone necklace must have given me the appearance of some kind of religious zealot. (I learned later from an Alaskan State Trooper that I had likely been profiled as an Irish terrorist.) Pulling me aside, the police subjected me to a thorough personal search. Two armed police were then commissioned as my personal escort. My attempts at banter met with a stony silence. Solemn faced they accompanied me to a magazine rack and waiting lounge. Fellow passengers stopped and stared. This silent escort remained in place for an hour until I boarded the jet bound for Alaska. They eventually left the suspicious, Alaska-bound, red-headed troublemaker at the walkway, and I ducked through the airplane doorway. I was safe; I was on my way to Alaska.

It was late at night when I arrived at my hotel in Anchorage. The following morning was my birthday. The message delivered under my hotel room door from Gary read: 'You are on flight #450 Hageland Air, International Airport, Concourse A-14. Leaves at 12:30 pm. Happy Birthday, Honey!'

I hailed a taxi to the local supermarket. My mission was to purchase fresh fruit and vegetables, a luxury out in the bush. Staggering around jetlagged, I stuffed the groceries into two children's clear plastic backpacks, the only suitable containers I could find in the sprawling supermarket.

With my luxury purchases in tow, I hailed a cab. We headed for the airport and pulled up outside the international lounge. 'Sorry, lady,' the cab driver said, pulling my bags out of the car's trunk and not looking at all sorry, 'Only one airport stop today. This is it.'

Slinging the bags of fruit over my shoulders, I plonked my backpack on the suitcase and proceeded to drag my heavy luggage into the building. It would be a long walk to the domestic lounge.

A wonderful stranger who heard me at the information counter had noticed my distress. I was trying to understand directions to concourse A-14. 'I can help. Follow me,' he said. His blue eyes twinkled as he took my fruit bags from me and ran the long corridors alongside me.

'Thank you *so* much,' I panted, 'I'm heading out to St Mary's. I'm scared I'll miss the flight!'

'No worries.' He grinned over his shoulder, 'I know where it is. Down that way. Far end of the corridor!' Hageland Air was, of course, at the *extreme* far end of the terminal. Our frantic arrival and the bags of fruit had drawn bemused looks from those quietly waiting. A mandatory public personal weigh in, then a bag weigh in, had shredded what was left of my dignity. We were asked to board immediately. They had been waiting for me, and the weather here could change quickly. When I glanced around to thank my anonymous guide, he had vanished.

The plane raced along the tarmac and lifted into the air. We soared away from any signs of civilisation and out into the vastness beyond. There were four rows of single seats on each side of the plane, separated by an aisle. I was the only female passenger. As we continued our ascent a scarcely audible American voice recording assured the eight passengers aboard of safety provisions.

'Should landing be necessary and unplanned, a gun and provisions are safely stored down the rear of the plane.' Really? 'Flares are in the nose.' I realised with slightly rising panic and dampening hands that it was a bit late now for lessons on how to load and fire a gun, let alone release a flare. Anyway, who would ever see a flare in this utter wilderness? And what was the gun to shoot for? To shoot terrorists? Fellow passengers grabbing too many provisions? Bears? On closer inspection I could see little black shapes moving in and out of scrub near the winding riverbeds. Bears.

The panorama of deep Alaska that exposed itself proudly to me was stunningly grandiose. Even if I had thought to pack a camera, I could see that any photo would only capture small slices of the vista and thus diminish the impact of all that lay before me. I felt like I had stepped into one of those large and minutely detailed oil paintings executed by a world famous artist, an artist with a rare talent for capturing the spirit of overwhelmingly vast and magnificent landscapes. Inside this vivid oil painting I was diminished to the size of a Lilliputian, breathless at the height and layers of jagged blue-and-white mountain ranges that towered around me, mountains that at times appeared so alarmingly close and then marched forever out of frame.

This was bush Alaska; the vast remote tracts of this huge state unreachable by road. Most of bush Alaska was home to Alaskan native people, many of whom still lived the subsistence way of life. These parts could only be reached by small airplane, and travel from place to place was typically by snow machine, boat, or dog sled.

The early afternoon September sunlight allowed unusually vibrant colours of brief autumn sunlight to grace the riverbeds. The low, softly mounded stretches of vegetation appeared to be an enormous finely crafted patchwork quilt – a quilt stitched by a country woman with a passion for deep aubergine, vivid gold, occasional scatterings of intense yellow green and long luxurious threads of silver blue. There was no particular pattern or direction. Each silver river thread ran into various points of the skilful design without causing disruption or distraction to the eye.

After an hour and a half of this spectacular journey, pages of the *Anchorage Daily News* had drifted to the aisle. The engines with their monotonous loud thrumming and vibrations had caused my fellow passengers to nod gradually off to sleep. They were missing it all.

A fog came upon us so softly, smudging the ground and misting the windows. The two pilots sitting immediately in front of us stopped their camaraderie and banter, and focused for the first time on actually flying the plane. They peered intently and silently into the deepening gloom in the apparent hope of seeing anything at all. There followed 20 minutes of intense brown swirling fog, while I kept starboard watch. Should a mountain peak suddenly loom into view, I would yell, 'Mountain to the right!' to save us from guns and flares. When I could finally see the wing tip again my eyes had dried, as I was too scared to blink and risk missing anything. Now I could relax; my watch was over.

As we emerged out of the thinning haze, the closeness of a sheer green hill to the wing tip caused me to lean forward and check nervously how far we were from the surrounding terrain. To my great surprise I saw man-made constructions; small wooden huts perched precariously on the lower hillsides.

I spoke out loud, mainly to warn the pilots in case they had missed them, 'Look at all the huts down there!'

A fellow passenger laughed, and others, awakening now, joined in. 'That's St Mary's,' he replied, amused. Our destination.

Chapter 2

Whanganui Childhood

I was born on the floor of the foyer at Burwood Hospital, Christchurch, in the South Island of New Zealand. My mother didn't have time to take off her coat. She was quite sure I was going to be born during the bumpy car ride to the hospital.

'You were easy,' she liked to tell me. 'Easy born and easy raised.'

When I was six weeks old my parents moved away from their Christchurch family base to Whanganui in the North Island. They had one piece of furniture, a small wooden stool. My father was a draftsman and needed to gain further training to become an architect. The position in Whanganui with the education board offered him that opportunity. We would be staying there for fourteen years.

My mother's large family was extremely close. Her father had died of a heart attack when I was a baby. He was an orphan who had been raised into a farming family. The holding he was given by the government on his return from the First World War was lost in the Great Depression.

His wife, my maternal grandmother, had been both a piano and a singing teacher. She came from a well-to-do family. My mother told us that even though she had been raised in the 'poor arm' of the family, it had been a happy and close one.

My mother and her siblings spent much of their childhood in South Canterbury. They would collect coal for their fire that had been dropped on the railway lines by passing trains. The family survived mostly on rabbits my grandfather shot. Their hut walls were lined with newspapers to keep out the cold southern winds that blew through the cracks. They would put stones in the oven to heat and hold them in their hands to stop them from freezing on their long walks to school.

There was always music at night. My grandmother loved to sing to them in a deep contralto voice. She particularly liked to sing Negro spirituals, and would roll her eyes and lower her head to meet her children's awe-struck gazes. 'I'm comin', I'm comin', though my head is hangin' looooooooow,' she would quaver at them as they sat clutching each other in fascinated horror.

An English talent scout discovered my grandmother singing at a local hall and offered to pay for her to go to London to study opera. At that time, she was pregnant with her fifth child. She had so desperately wanted to go that she had tried to abort the baby by jumping off a kitchen chair. 'I *tried*, but it never worked. That's why your sister has my voice,' she would tell her children later, looking tenderly at my aunt.

That sister was the one born after my mother. She remained my mother's closest friend in the world. My grandmother had instructed my mother to look after her always. Throughout their years living at home they shared a bed. They both grew their strange little toenails into hooks and would use them to have 'hen fights' at night in bed, each vying for more mattress space. My grandmother had told her seven children, 'Always remember you come from very good stock.' My mother and aunt would giggle, and reply, 'Yeah, chicken stock.'

My grandmother's visits to us in Whanganui were always colourful. There was much excitement when she visited. My grandmother, whom we called Ma, would take over the cooking. I was amazed to see her actually elbow my mother away from the kitchen sink. One day she picked up one of our chooks and lopped off its head with an axe. The chook ran headless around the backyard while we screamed in terror. Ma would also drink home-brewed beer with my father. She would listen avidly to the radio, especially when the horse races and rugby games were on. Her younger brother had been an All Black.

My mother told me later that Ma always slipped a silver coin under the plate when she left. 'To help out. You need it.' There was nothing quiet and religious about my maternal grandmother at all. It was such a contrast to the prayers and manners displayed when my father's parents visited.

My father's parents were Methodists. His mother had been strict Brethren before marrying my grandfather, who was a lay minister in the Methodist church. This grandmother had also been a missionary in Fiji.

'Growing up in such a religious family,' my father would declare, 'has put me off churches for*ever*.' He would thump the table in time with 'ever.'

'Why?' I ventured one day when I was old enough to think about it.

'Because every *penny* (thump) my father earned went to the *church* (thump)! My brother and I *never* (thump) saw my parents while growing up. All their time *and* money went to the *church* (loud thump)'!

There were only two boys in that family, and my father was the eldest. His mother had suffered severe post-natal depression when my uncle was born and had to be sent away. She had spent months knitting baby girl's clothes in readiness for a daughter. She had wanted a girl so badly that she continued to dress my uncle in a frock and bonnet when she came back.

'We *never* saw them.' My father was still angry. 'It was always *church, church, church*,' After the thumping had finished he would move distractedly to the kitchen cupboard where he kept some alcohol. Standing, he would pour himself a small whisky, while his eyes chased painful distant memories. 'You know in their hour of need not one person from the church showed any concern . . . at all.' With one swig, the glass would be emptied and banged on the bench. Then he would go and get his pipe. Brooding. All his life he would hide the wine or whisky in the top cupboard of the kitchen, fearful that his parents might discover there was alcohol in the house.

When these grandparents came to visit us in Whanganui, they would head south out of Whanganui to Ratana Pa. The Ratana movement had become a new strand of Christianity based on the Maori prophet TW Ratana's teachings. Ratana was a faith healer and the Ratana church had been ordained in New Zealand in 1925. It was open to people from all denominations but had a particularly close affiliation with the Methodist church.

One day, several months after our arrival in Whanganui, my paternal grandparents paid us a visit. After they had attended the Sunday morning Methodist church service everyone piled into my grandfather's car and we headed up the Whanganui River for a picnic.

We stopped at a lush green knoll 40 kilometres up the river. The group set out picnic rug and food. My two-year-old sister was playing in the grass, clutching my grandfather's hand. My grandmother cradled me in her arms. I was dressed in Sunday finery. My mother had clothed me in the silk baby's dress that had originally been my sister's, given to her by my grandparents for her christening.

We had not long stopped, when a young Maori woman approached the group. She had seen our car. Visitors up the river were not very common in those days. My grandparents were very welcoming. They had had regular contact with Maori in Whanganui, so they stood and greeted her in Maori.

'Kia ora, tena koe,' said my grandmother.

'Tena koutou,' the woman responded, smiling shyly at them and nodding at my parents. She had seen the group setting up their picnic from Koriniti Pa on the riverbank below. She tentatively approached my grandmother, who was holding me in her arms. 'Like a princess!' She breathed in wonder at my fine frock. 'I hold her?' My grandmother carefully passed me over.

'Tou ingoa?' my grandmother asked her, wanting to know her name.

'Ko Edna au.' She smiled again, 'I take her down there?' She nodded in the direction of the pa.

My grandmother looked at my mother. My mother was a bit in awe of her and didn't argue. 'I used to be a bit scared of your nana you know, dear,' my mother told me. 'But it was silly really. She was such a *good* woman.'

My grandmother nodded to Edna and reassured my parents. 'She will be fine. God is good.'

So Edna took me down to Koriniti Pa. We were gone a couple of hours before she brought me back. Edna was smiling.

'Happy. Tino pai. Very good.' I had charmed them all. I was sound asleep in her arms. 'Ka hoki ano koutou? Come back?' she asked them, glancing at my mother. They all nodded.

'Ae, we'll be back,' said my grandmother.

Six months later when my grandparents returned, the family picnicked again near Koriniti Pa. My grandparents had spent the morning filling their suitcases with pumice from Castlecliff Beach. They would give away the pumice stone to everyone in the church on their return.

Edna saw us and again climbed up the road to join our group.

'My little princess,' she said holding out her arms for me. This time she was away much longer down in the pa, but my mother said they had not been at all worried. Edna was lovely. I was a good baby. Easy. Edna brought me back content and asleep again. She told them she had a job at the post office in town.

'Please, your address? I visit?' My father wrote our address down for her.

'Edna used to bike to our place to visit you,' said my mother, 'right up until you started school.'

I was told this story for the first time on my 45th birthday during a brief trip home from Sydney. I had recently been christened in the Maori Anglican church in Redfern.

'You know,' my father said, 'we tried several times to have you christened when you were growing up. Your sister and brother were both christened.' My brother had been born five years after me. 'Nana and Grandpa insisted.'

Mum raised her eyebrows and exchanged a small smile with Dad. She continued the story. 'But every time we arranged it, you became ill. Measles, chicken pox . . .' She looked pleased with me. 'Always something.'

'It seems quite amazing to us that you have now been baptised into the Maori church,' Dad finished.

Their story was all a bit surprising to me. It was making more sense of what happened to me. I had been drawn to Maori throughout my childhood in Whanganui and again in my teaching in Christchurch. I had at times wondered why. Did we have Maori blood perhaps? I had also had some unusual Maori spiritual experiences. Experiences I had not shared with my parents.

'We've watched you for many years and you seem to be drawn to those Maoris,' my father said, holding out three presents. 'Your grandparents would have been very proud of you.' I wasn't so sure that he was.

I remembered a Christchurch visit to my paternal grandparents when I was eight. My grandfather and I had been very close. One morning he had taken me to see the carving of the ridgepole for Rehua marae that was being built. He had worked closely with the carvers through the Methodist mission and was chairman of the Rehua committee.

I was told before entering the workplace that it was a great privilege to be invited there, especially as a female. They allowed it because I was so young. My grandfather and a Maori man had said prayers first. Then they opened a small wooden door and I stepped into the room. They followed me.

The carvers were chipping away on a long beam that ran the length of a large shed. I could smell the newly cut wood and hear the quiet sound of constant chiselling. I remembered how friendly my grandfather was with the men. How welcoming they were to me. In my memory the room was golden with light.

My father interrupted my reverie. 'We've decided to give you these things.' He passed me a small woven reed basket. 'My mother was given this during her missionary time in Fiji.'

The kete was very finely woven and old. My father continued. 'This,' he said, passing me a long carved stick, 'this was your grandfather's walking stick.' I recognised it immediately as my grandfather's tokotoko. My grandfather always carried the stick. He said it gave him strength. He had walked into the Whanganui bush during one of his visits to Ratana Pa and found the stick on the forest bed. It was just after the end of World War Two. He had sat in the bush on a log and carved 'Koromiko 1945' on it.

'And this,' my father grinned at me, 'this is a Maori bible that belonged to your grandfather. We've had it rebound to give to you.' The bible was dated 1860 and there was an inscription to me in it. I was shocked. My father was giving me a bible? Wow. This was very special and unusual.

To celebrate this gift giving, my parents performed a song for me. My parents had always made music together. They were both very musical. My mother had taught herself the guitar when I was growing up. My father played the mouth organ, double bass and beer bottle trumpet. I used to fall asleep listening to their music all through my years at home. Our whole family sang together in the car; we harmonised drying the dishes at night and often had musical evenings. It had been a poor but happy childhood.

Mum picked up her guitar and Dad harmonised with her. He added special parts with his mouth organ. Together they played for me, 'You must have been a beautiful baby.'

Chapter 3

First Encounters

We landed on the stony strip at St Mary's and unfolded ourselves from the cramped plane. Carefully picking our way across the muddy ground we entered the 'airport', a small wooden hut standing in the middle of nowhere. Couples and elders in heavily padded *quspuks*, traditional quilted smocks, sat along the wooden benches that lined three sides of the dimly lit room. The counter was on the fourth side.

This was my first introduction to the culture and it became an unforgettable memory of the Eskimo people. I took a seat quietly against the wall and tried not to stare. The people had a soft roundness to them; there was a faint smell of fish oil in the air.

The room was gloomy. Dull sunshine filtered through a small dirty window. There were about six people in the room all interacting with each other, smiling and nodding. Small children played around their feet on the dusty floor. My problem was I could not hear a sound. I thought I must have lost my hearing on the plane.

One woman leaned forward to the child on the floor and motioned with her head. The child stood and went to sit by an elder. The elder remained motionless staring ahead.

Minutes later another child joined the first. They turned to each other and, raising their shoulders in a kind of conspiratorial giggle, they lent forward together. The second child took a small plastic toy from his *quspuk* pocket, and showed it to his friend. The other child took it and turned it over and over in his hands examining it from every angle. Not one word was spoken. I later learned that much communication is done by facial expression and body gesture, that children are taught from a very young age to be quiet, so as not to scare the game away. It was peaceful, but unnerving.

Eventually I was called for. A pilot in a woollen hat and Carhartts padded overalls appeared, carrying a clipboard and sporting a few days beard growth. 'Stevens, Tutalgaq?' I could hear *him* clearly. I stood self-consciously. All eyes turned to assess this tall red headed *gussaq* as she walked out of the room with exaggerated nonchalance, as if she made this plane journey every day.

'Hop up the front with me.' The pilot grinned. The plane was a two seater so there wasn't much choice. I stepped off the wing into the cockpit and sank down in the small bucket seat. I tried to find which belt latched where. 'Here, take these!' He handed me a pair of headphones with earmuffs. He turned the ignition switch and the plane fired into life.

As we lifted and flew along the riverbeds and between the low hills, I was relieved to discover an instrument depicting the height from the terrain below on the dashboard in front. I wouldn't need to worry if we hit more fog. We flew a lot lower this time, winding along riverbeds. We were flying over the colourful tundra. The rivers here appeared to be even more profuse and split. They snaked in all directions below us. I could not contain my amazement.

'Look at all the rivers!' I exclaimed.

The pilot lifted his headset and turning to me drawled, 'Excuse me?'

'Look at all the rivers!' I repeated my exclamation with my mouth mocking amazement. He grinned.

'That's *one* river, honey!' Chuckling at my naivety he replaced his headphones and returned to his concentration. I remained pink and silent for the remainder of the flight. Of course, I should have known it. I was seeing the tributaries of the mighty Yukon River. A river that snaked over 3000 kilometres from its source in British Colombia Canada, across the Yukon territory through Alaska and all the way out to the Bering Sea.

Eventually I looked down upon a steep bluff where the hilltop was tattooed with a long dark stripe. I could make out a red ute parked there. As we suddenly dropped to land along that strip and skidded to a stop alongside the truck, I could see Gary. The stiff crosswind had whipped his tie from within his heavy jacket. It waved gaily at me, a symbol of a civilisation far distant from this lone outpost in this deep valley along the mighty Yukon River.

Gary leaned on the ute's dusty tray, grinning casually as if I arrived every afternoon from New Zealand to this point deep in bush Alaska.

Tutalgaq, with its population of 500, was about eight times smaller than Balclutha. As the ute bumped its way down the rough track to the faculty housing, I was shocked at the old plastic bags drifting across the road from a smouldering dump.

Gary had my hand clasped firmly in his. 'I have so missed you, babe!'

I was very grateful at this chance to be reunited with Gary two months after he had left New Zealand. Mr Mark, my boss, who had been so supportive of us, had urged me to go. He was a man fond of the outdoors himself, and like most men, Alaska appealed to him as the ultimate in adventure. One day in July my boss had asked me, 'Emma, when are you going to visit?'

'Christmas holidays,' I replied.

'Christmas! Why aren't you going in the September holidays?' New Zealand schools had a two-week spring break late September to early October.

'Because it will take me so long to get there and back I won't have time to stay for more than a few days. It's too far and too expensive for that.'

Mr Mark grinned. 'Well, why don't you ask me for some leave then?' Leave. I hadn't thought of that.

'Could I please have some leave to visit Gary in Pilot Station these coming holidays?'

'You have a month,' he chuckled.

So here I was. Strong, earthy, pungent smells wafted from the ground and hung in drifting reminders of this land as I stepped out of the ute. We clambered up the six rough-cast iron steps and opened the door. This was the principal's new housing. The smell of new paint and carpet was overwhelming. The large enclosed entrance porch had rows of hooks suspended above a long heater centimetres above the vinyl flooring. Plenty of room here to hang coats and stack boots for drying.

Opening the door beyond, we slipped out of our shoes and stepped into the lounge. The place was warm and cosy. Central heating in *gussaq* housing was mandatory to attract teachers to these outposts of civilisation.

Gary carried the bags across the thick new carpet and placed the backpacks of food carefully on the bench. He returned to the lounge window where I stared out across the valley. He wrapped his arms around me.

I could see out across the track where the occasional four-wheeler buzzed past. The riders were well padded against the brisk cold; boxes and children were stacked on front and back. Across a small gully, thin trails of smoke rose in the air from a cluster of small huts. The little red, green and white dwellings nestled in among the trees looked as if a giant's hand had thrown them down. Rather than sitting in neat rows, they sat higgledy-piggledy on the hillside.

Tall conifers ran along the ridge above and merged with other shrubs as far as the eye could see. Below and to the right, stunted yellowing aspens seemed particularly calming and subtle in their informal arrangements. All was serene and still.

'Wow, I could *live* here!' I exclaimed, surprised at my intense reaction. Gary hugged me again. He chuckled. I had always said, 'Who'd want to live in *Alaska*?'

'Yeah, amazing isn't it.' We both stared out the window together.

'You know,' I repeated more slowly, 'I really could imagine myself living here.' There was a long pause.

'Are you serious?' Gary turned me around to face him.

I grinned. 'Yes. This is so much better than I imagined. It's beautiful, stunning, breathtaking . . .' I trailed off as I saw his serious expression.

'You know if you *do* want to come out here to live with me, you'll promise me one thing?' He was looking extremely serious. Not delighted at all.

'What?' I was smiling at his earnestness. I was also feeling washed with excitement at this radical new plan. I wanted him to get enthusiastic too.

'You'll promise me that we *will* go home again, won't we?' Gary had always referred to New Zealand as home. It had always felt like home to him.

'Yes, of course!' I reassured him with a hug. I was surprised that he was seriously worried I might not want to return to New Zealand. He knew what New Zealand meant to me.

I had to admit I was surprised at myself as well. Here was I now contemplating leaving New Zealand again after so long living in Sydney, and having only recently returned to my home country. But I really did want to come back here to Alaska. Fancy that!

Gary had warned me of the 'Alaska effect'. After living in Alaska for twelve years he had seen the impact this landscape could have on first time visitors. People either hated it or loved it, there was no middle road.

I loved it.

Chapter 4

Homesick in Sydney

My previous upheaval and move had occurred only three years earlier. My 20-year old daughter Ella and I had lived in Sydney for eleven years, and I had wanted to go home. Ella was managing a job and her own income. After years of struggle we were starting to plan ahead.

In the end I left Sydney quite suddenly. It had been a hot fine October day. I had been washing the car outside on the concrete pad behind the apartment block. In the distance I heard a phone's muffled ring. I stopped and listened. It was coming from my apartment on the ground floor. I turned off the hose and ran back carefully through the Lino-covered foyer to avoid slipping. I burst into my flat, but the phone had stopped. There was a message flashing on the answer phone. A message I had been waiting for.

That night when Ella came in from work I told her. 'Sweetheart, Life Education Trust New Zealand left me a message on the phone this morning.'

'Uh huh.' She looked up. Ella was aware I had been looking for jobs in New Zealand. We needed to move out of our apartment and rent it if we wanted to keep it. The mortgage repayments were killing me.

'They told me if I was serious in the application, they would appreciate meeting me for an interview.'

'Really! What about experience?' Ella asked. My problem was that

I had been gone for eleven years and was unfamiliar with the New Zealand curriculum. Finding a teaching job was difficult without recent New Zealand teaching experience.

'No worries, it includes training. The job is based in Dunedin.' Dunedin, in the Otago region, was the second largest city in the South Island. It was a six-hour drive north to where family were living in Christchurch. Ella and I agreed that I would move to a place where access was easy and cheap for us to fly back and forth. With budget airline Freedom Air flying into Dunedin, and family in Christchurch, Otago had seemed sensible.

'Can you afford the trip?' She looked at me carefully. We could read each other very clearly. We'd been through so much together. No point in fudging the truth.

'Yeah, I checked. I can do it. Flights are quite cheap. Holiday pay is coming up. This could be the one opportunity to get work back home.' I would ask for three days leave.

'I think you should go.' She gave me a little grin. 'I've seen a small apartment at Potts Point near Dad's place. No pets though.'

'Oh.' It was good she was looking, but we both knew she would love to keep Bel, her little Tenterfield terrier, with her. It would have been perfect if Ella could have stayed on in our apartment and had a flatmate to help pay off the rent. That way she could have kept Bel with her.

However the mortgage repayments were still way beyond anything Ella would be able to manage, even with a flatmate. We knew in order to keep our flat I would need to aim at a much higher rental market.

Finding Ella an apartment in inner Sydney at a reasonable rent that allowed animals on the premises had also proved impossible. We knew. We'd been looking for a while. So it was decided I would take Bel to New Zealand with me.

Ella had recently landed a job for a fashion house as a house model.

'Mum, I know I can manage the rent with this job,' she reassured me.

After all these years of our mutual dependence, I knew I would never leave if I didn't leave now. I was so homesick for New Zealand. After eleven years in this Australian city with its people, noise and heat, I had so longed for the peace of home and the cooler and richer greens of the New Zealand landscape.

Two days before leaving Sydney for my interview in Dunedin, a whole host of jobs suddenly appeared on the *New Zealand Education Gazette* website. They were newly created positions for Resource Teachers of Learning and Behaviour, and they offered advanced study and on-the-job training. I was currently working in Sydney as an Itinerant Teacher of Learning and Behaviour. These jobs seemed designed with me in mind.

Frantically I sent off emails to the positions advertised in and around Dunedin. I described my current work. I explained my imminent arrival in Dunedin and the three days I would be there.

Responses were fast and positive. I would be travelling from one interview to another. Five for resource teacher positions and one for the Life Education Trust. Six interviews in two days!

I could stay with a friend's family I had met through the Maori community in Sydney. Their offer included the use of a car and driver if I wanted one.

I called Ella from Dunedin after the interviews were done. 'Every one was great, dar, but I really liked the job at Balclutha. It comes with a teacher's flat. It's quiet, cheap rent, and I can have a pet!'

'Ooh, great!' Ella sounded excited too.

'Balclutha is also rural and peaceful,' I enthused. 'And so cool. You know they were growing roses in the garden beds around the school!' I so missed the roses. 'It's only about an hour from Dunedin airport. It's an easy and beautiful country drive. I know you'd love it.'

In Sydney, city schools and their problems were exhausting. Driving through heavy traffic from one city schoolyard problem to another had been draining. But now I would be travelling the beautiful countryside of the South East Otago region, visiting small country schools spread well apart by rolling green hills.

'Good, Mum.' There was finality in Ella's voice. I knew Ella was not as enthusiastic as me about country life. She was much more a city girl. She had decided she definitely did not want to come back with me.

'The Education Department will pay for my study leave, along with a school based office.' I paused for full effect. '*And* they'll give me my own computer and internet access from home for study!'

'Wow! You could finish your degree.' Ella sounded relieved. I'd dropped my studies two years earlier. I couldn't concentrate on extramural work. I was too preoccupied about managing financially, trying to keep our heads above rapidly rising money worries.

A few days after returning from the job interviews, I received multiple offers of employment as a New Zealand resource teacher in the Otago region. In the end, the Life Education Trust was the only job I had missed out on. I wrote a letter of resignation from my Sydney position and signed the Balclutha contract.

The following week I received the information pack about the job. 'Oh, look, I also get a removal allowance,' I read to Ella. '$NZ5000!'

We grinned together. I was financially stretched to the point of desperation, and did not want to sell the flat – our only anchor in a tide of upheaval.

Four years earlier and three months after buying the flat, my husband had suddenly left. I had struggled on with the mortgage alone, not on the double income that it was based upon, but on my own single income. I was desperate to cling to our only home and maintain some form of stability for Ella and myself in a world where the ground had moved beneath us.

Chapter 5

A Home in the Bush

Gary woke me the next morning with a cup of tea. He needed to leave for school.

'Honey, I've been thinking,' he began. 'If you truly are serious about coming back to live here,' I nodded, 'then I think we should try and arrange a meeting for you in Mountain Village while you're here.'

Mountain Village was a large village further downstream on the Yukon River. It was the central hub village that housed all district operations for the eleven village schools that made up the Lower Yukon School District.

'Maybe the superintendent could find me a job here too?'

Gary nodded seriously. This was a big change in our plans. I would need to get an immigration visa. And what about my Balclutha job? My stuff? Bel?

Jetlagged, I fell asleep again till late morning. Once awake and fully alert, I was still excited about my earlier decision and curious about everything. Now I wanted to check out the house. Teacher housing was mostly basic, and many villages had difficulty drawing in teachers to live in their primitive and uncomfortable conditions. The new housing block here had been a draw card for Gary. As part of a duplex, the house had a separate main entrance, but shared a common laundry utility room that housed the oil furnace for heating. The single back porch door led out of this utility area and down steps into a steep hillside.

There were three large bedrooms designed to host the many visitors from district office on school-related business that would expect to stay with the principal. The one bathroom included a large bathtub and overhead shower as well as the flush toilet that Gary warned me about. The vacuum pump that suctioned sewage was reminiscent of the noisy airplane toilets that made a terrific din on the flush. It took some nerve to push the flush button as the sound reverberated loudly around the house. No discreet toileting here, but compared to the many other village houses in the bush where honey buckets or 55-gallon drums were the only option, a real toilet was a welcome addition. I was secretly pleased. Honey buckets needed regular carting and emptying into village sewage areas, or were left in their frozen state till they thawed in spring. I knew this bathroom was luxurious by comparison.

Floor panel heating vents hugged the skirting boards in every room. The windows were small and triple-glazed, opening up and out from the top or side. There were mosquito screens on every one. The mosquitoes and 'no-seeum' bugs that tormented both people and game animals throughout the short summers and fall were often described as the true Alaskan Air Force. 'Alaska windows, honey,' said Gary.

The spacious kitchen/dining area opened into the lounge. Along one wall in the dining room was an expansive four-door pantry, essential for storing large quantities of food during the long winter months.

On the other side of the kitchen, a door gave access to the common utility area that housed the furnace, two upright freezers, two washing machines and two dryers. The utility area was designed for ease of access for maintenance of the furnace, critical in plunging temperatures. Tim and Anna, our young teaching neighbours, were a bright young couple from Seattle who loved the outdoors. Tim taught high school science and Anna was an elementary teacher.

Our house boasted brand new furniture. Gary had already sent me photos, so the reality was familiar and reassuring. There were also several boxes of household effects that Gary had bought from the previous school principal, Jared, for a nominal amount.

Jared and his family had decided to move back down to South Carolina for family reasons. Like most outward-bound teachers, Jared found it much easier to sell the items on to someone in the village who needed them. An incoming teacher could afford them. It was cheaper than paying for the expense of trying to ship them out. 'Fly or float' were the only transport options.

I started unpacking the boxes. I uncovered an array of treasures that included kitchen crockery and cutlery, placemats and serviettes, pots and pans, bread maker, microwave, vacuum cleaner and complete bedding for three rooms.

As I unpacked Gary walked in for lunch. It was so lovely to have him walk back through the door in an everyday way.

'What have you been up to, honey?' he asked.

'Look what's here.' I showed him the collapsible shelves, a television, a stereo system and two telephones. I was pleased to be starting some home decorating. The place needed it. I stood up. Time to get some lunch.

'Don't forget to stay away from the tap water,' he reminded me again. 'Boiling is safest.'

Over lunch I asked Gary about the food we had. I was planning on taking over the cooking now I was here. We walked into the laundry area and he showed me our freezer. The two freezers stood side by side, and could be locked, but it wasn't necessary. I was reminded of the importance of food and survival.

Gary had ordered in some meat in anticipation of my arrival. It had been shipped out as part of a cheaper combined bulk order by the faculty. It came from a butcher in Anchorage who specialised in providing meat to bush villages with *gussaq* teachers. Our freezer was packed with meat wrapped in butcher's paper, deeply frozen and labelled, 'pork roast x 1', 'beefsteaks x 6' and so on. I was relieved there didn't appear to be any of the moose meat that I knew was part of the regular diet. I wasn't sure I was ready for that yet.

I grabbed one of the frozen chickens. That might be good for dinner. 'Are there any potatoes?' Flaked potatoes filled with additives were popular with many American households, but real whole potatoes were often rotten here, sometimes frozen in the middle and always old. They were a great luxury. I would not be eating many potatoes out in the bush.

It was the same with fresh vegetables and fruit. During the short warmer-weather time frame above zero degrees, when fresh fruit and vegetables do not freeze, someone could carry them directly to you on their flight out, but they would have to prioritise their relatively heavy weight over any other item that may be needed within their 30lb personal limit. I had been 99lbs overweight on my baggage check-in at Anchorage. That had cost me $US99. So fresh fruit and vegetables were usually an unaffordable luxury. I had brought along a bag of carrots from the supermarket without a second thought. When I considered now how much they actually ended up costing me, I viewed them quite differently.

As a special treat for my visit, Gary had ordered a bag of potatoes and fresh milk flown in from the nearest large hub city, Bethel. This had cost a further $US30, more than $NZ45, an expensive treat. Instead of wasting money on such luxuries, Gary regularly used rice instead of potatoes. He also chose deep frozen vegetables instead of fresh and, at the price we had now paid for them, I was definitely going to follow suit.

I spent the rest of the day sleeping, cooking and staring out the windows scarcely believing I was actually here on the Lower Yukon. This new plan hung over me. It changed the context of everything I had decided. I was now going to return to New Zealand and resign from my job at the end of this school year. The resource teacher job that I loved so much had provided everything I needed – great climate, easy access to my daughter in Sydney, ability to visit family by road and opportunities to immerse myself back in the Maori culture. Was I really planning to give all that up for this?

I thought about my last move from Sydney three years earlier. Now I would have to face all that packing and reorganising of my life once again.

Chapter 6

Farewell Sydney

Three years earlier, when I had decided to take up the job in New Zealand, there seemed to be so much to do before I could leave my Sydney apartment. Sorting. Discarding. And I was teaching full time. Luckily the summer school holidays started early December and one of my friends worked as a real estate agent.

'I'll be happy to manage your place,' she told me over coffee on Saturday morning. 'I'll make sure we get excellent tenants. Being so close to the city, it'll lease easily, and for a good price.' I would still need to top up the mortgage repayments with my NZ income, but I wouldn't have to sell it yet. Right then, I just had to focus on emptying and sorting. On packing and shipping, and on settling Ella.

'Haere ra e hoa. Farewell.' Members of the Maori church in Redfern, part of the Maori community in Sydney, had become a supportive group of close friends that had embraced me during these past years. I had arrived at the church the year my marriage ended, desperate for a feeling of home and belonging.

I had had a series of premonitions leading up to my contact with the church and I was looking for elders to talk to about these. The elders had embraced me and not judged. I was taken in with much love/aroha. Maori accepted my gifts as quite normal. They said it was the gift of 'seeing', of 'matakite'. To me it felt more like the ability to inadvertently lock onto someone's energy field and read it.

My family, especially my mother and my aunt, had had a bit of history with such 'odd occurrences'. My aunt would have dreams and feelings, but my mother's experiences were more in daily life.

Once a strange woman had knocked on my mother's door. 'Can you help me, I've lost my car keys in the park,' she exclaimed, waving at the large park across the road from our house.

My mother said later, 'I know it was a bit strange, but I just said to her, "Come with me." I led her right into the middle of the park, straight to the lost keys lying in a bed of short grass!' The woman was very grateful.

'Wasn't that amazing,' my Mum wondered. 'We're a bit funny like that in the family. Must be the gypsy blood.' Although they had discovered no proof for their strongly held belief, my mother and her sister were both convinced that a strain of gypsy blood satisfactorily explained the peculiar events that they both experienced from time to time.

I used to discuss this with Paratai, a kuia (elder) in the Maori community in Sydney. We were drawn together, she and I, from the start. She loved to tell me about the first time she saw me. 'There was something about you, darling. You'd been in another world. I could feel it.' Paratai was a tutor in te reo, the Maori language, and I had found myself learning the language again. Paratai watched out for me and gave me lessons in protocol, language and life.

'Come on darling, get up and sing.' She'd nudge me and pull me to my feet, giving me absolutely no choice in the matter. Or 'Come on – clear up time,' and she would stand and start gathering dishes. She would motion me with her head to follow. Sometimes it seemed rude to clean up when men were giving speeches. 'Don't worry,' she'd say with a laugh when we reached the relative distance of the kitchen. 'That man'll go on for hours.'

Paratai never seemed to stop working. She was always preparing gifts of food, or hand cream she'd make up at home and pour into bottles for this person or that. Home remedies for flu as well. Big preserving bottles of vaguely brown fluid that contained grated ginger. I had never been a recipient of that, but I knew how to make it.

Paratai was also my protector. 'Watch out for that one, darling,' she would whisper during someone's long speech. 'He's too full of himself.'

The Maori community included a special choir that I sang in. The choir was a tight-knit group that travelled everywhere together. We had mid-week practices and sang at special ceremonies throughout the city. I had helped make everyone korowai, cloaks, to wear at our performances. I felt at one with the group. Lorraine, one of the choir members and I were strong alto singers.

'E hoa, you're off the note,' she would nudge me when she made a mistake. We always poked each other in the ribs if we thought one of us was on the wrong note. We did it when we heard others off key as well. Together we thought we were indestructible. It made for much giggling and enjoyment.

The Maori community held a farewell hakari or feast for me one week before my departure in early January. Amongst their farewell gifts was a rug to keep my knees warm and a thermos for those long southern country drives. They sang for me and I wept.

'Ka nui nga mihi aroha kia koutou katoa,' I replied, acknowledging their thoughtfulness and love. I would sorely miss them all, especially Paratai. Many were jealous of me going home. It was close to all of our hearts. Something we often talked about.

'You can buy marshmallow and chocolate Easter eggs there, remember,' Lorraine had laughed. She always brought back bags of them when she visited. 'Go the All Blacks!' They all understood my excitement. There were kisses and tears.

My Sydney-born friends were far more worried. 'You are going *where?*'

'How big?'

'What restaurants?'

'Are you *serious*? The country!' For them it was all too sudden. Too sudden and too small.

I tried to explain. 'This job in Balclutha is offering me a chance to step out of all this financial pressure. It's a chance to reinvent my life.' I knew what I wanted. I wanted the quiet, cool and peaceful country life. I wanted to cook meat freely without offending my vegetarian daughter.

'I want to pick roses from my garden and to sleep without being woken by heavy traffic and sticky heat.' I laughed. 'I also want to travel to work without stopping and starting at 21 traffic lights each morning!' I wanted time to look after myself.

On the day the packers arrived it was hot, and I was sitting on the floor in Ella's bedroom sorting through another pile of papers. Bel had been lying on the bed. She jumped down and yelped. She was dragging herself around. It looked like her back legs were paralysed. I snatched her up in my arms and ran out through the living room.

'I'm taking my dog to the vet!' I called to the startled men standing amongst swathes of packing paper and boxes. I ran outside without stopping to put on my shoes. Barefoot I ran the three blocks to the local vet on the main highway. I had been there the week before sorting out the shots Bel needed for her to journey to New Zealand.

'Help me!' was all I could sob as I thrust Bel at the receptionist. 'I don't know what happened. I think she's paralysed!' The woman took Bel out the back. Eventually the vet appeared and questioned me more about what I'd seen.

'I've given her a shot to sedate her,' he told me sympathetically. 'I'll watch her overnight and see what happens. Do prepare yourself that we may need to put her down.' I nodded dumbly. Losing Bel at this stressful time of parting would be unbearable.

The following day Ella and I went back to the vet. We had hardly slept. Bel had become the vessel of our separation angst. She was much better and was moving. X-rays showed she had lower back problems. A slipped disc. All that jumping against a car restrainer had probably done it.

Bel had been the perfect pet, except for separation anxiety when we got out of the car. She would bark and frantically leap all over the seats. Recently I had bought her a small seat-belt harness. Straining against it had probably caused this back injury. A few days later and after hundreds of dollars paid out in bills we brought her home. She'd also had her heart-worm vaccination for the flight.

Home was a wreck of sold furniture and piles of stuff to go to Ella's flat. I had a few days to try to keep Bel sedated and quiet. Another close friend from the Maori choir leant me an old dog cage she had used for flying her dogs back and forth to NZ. I put Bel in that. I was exhausted with all this to the point of collapse.

When I left Sydney airport, Ella and a girlfriend came to farewell me. It was very sad. We watched through the airport window as the little crate with Bel inside trundled up the baggage conveyor belt onto the plane. Ella and I focused our tears on Bel. It was too hard to farewell each other, even for a short time. I hugged her hard.

'I'll be back in July for your 21st,' I reminded us both. She nodded, trying to look brave. I turned and walked quickly through the departure gate. I could not look back.

Chapter 7

Out and About

After yet another sleep in and lunch the following day, I sloshed down the muddy hill to Pilot Station School. I was wearing the Blueband Kiwi gumboots I had brought with me. My first thoughts on waking were of the arrangements I'd have to make when I got back to New Zealand. Where would I store my belongings? Who'd look after Bel? How on earth could I farewell my family again? We had talked about it over dinner the night before.

'You know it'll mean applying for a work visa and residency, honey,' Gary said. 'With 9/11 on everyone's minds, that could take a while.' I nodded. Paperwork was always hard. I remembered my ordeal at LA airport. Maybe they had noted me as 'a potential terrorist' and would refuse me residency.

'Then you'll have to sit the Alaskan qualifying exams, in order to get teaching certification here.' No Child Left Behind, the new national standards initiative had just become law in the US, so this would be an added pressure. I had completed my masters degree just two weeks earlier. I pushed the thought of more study to the back of my mind.

The reality of yet another huge life change was lost in the captivating landscape I stared at through the lounge room window. I knew I definitely wanted to live here in bush Alaska with Gary. I'd overcome hurdles before. I could do it again.

I plodded on down the hill, wondering if there were any bears around. Gary had warned me, 'Never run from a bear. Just make yourself as large as you can.' Apparently bears had poor eyesight. 'Wave your arms out to the sides, or grab a stick and wave it.' I had been told that there were brown bears around here. 'If you see one, don't panic,' Gary reminded me. 'Put your head down and back away. Whatever you do, don't run.'

I had read some gruesome stories about those foolish enough to try to outrun a bear. Bears do not usually attack humans, but it is particularly dangerous ever to get between a mother and her cub. Attacks could be fast and ferocious. One rake of those claws won't leave much flesh behind. As big and cumbersome as they might appear, bears can run fast. Speeds of up to 30 miles per hour are common.

Black bears are not feared as much as the brown or grizzly, but Gary told me the native people speak little of either. It is one animal never hunted for meat, as it is considered less than pure. Bears hibernate in the winter but hunt for salmon, moose and caribou in spring, summer and autumn. They also graze on the abundant berries in the summer and autumn months, the blackberries, blueberries, cranberries and salmon berries. Alaska is a smorgasbord of tasty food delights for bears. I had seen them foraging from the plane.

Pilot Station school was on two campuses. The secondary school was on the upper campus close to us, the primary school was down the bottom of the hill. The schools were separated by a muddy track. There was much excitement about the impending prospect of one site for both schools. The building was going on day and night in the compound on the hill above our house.

As I climbed up the long flight of wooden steps from the track up into the administration office, I was reminded of the outside of a shearing shed I had once visited in back country Otago. It had the same red painted walls with trim made of peeling white paint. The entrance was caked in dried mud and dirt. No one bothered taking shoes or boots off here.

Gary's secretary Mary and the business officer Anthea sat behind large desks in the entryway. Towering files were stacked on the floor and on their desks. They smiled shyly when I walked in. Gary had taught me the Yup'ik word for Hello. '*Waqaa*.' I could speak some Maori, and the vowel sounds were similar. I loved trying out new words.

Gary had always had an excellent rapport with the native Alaskans he worked with. He found it easy to listen and learn from them, and was not afraid to laugh at himself. This is an attribute highly regarded in many indigenous cultures, and was one of the things that had attracted me to him.

In Tutalgaq he was already well respected by the natives who worked for him, as well as many of the elders that he took time to stop and talk to. I need not have worried at all. As soon as I smiled and said '*Waqaa*,' there were fits of giggles between Mary and Anthea.

'Please say some English words, you speak funny!' We all joined in the laughter.

Throughout my visit I was told over and again how much the people loved hearing my Kiwi accent.

Mary and Anthea wore the traditional *quspuk*, a one-piece, loose-fitting dress with long sleeves, hood and a large pocket in the front. For the men the top stopped at hip level. The women had a frilled ruffle around the knees and the length dropped to the mid calf or ankle. The borders of the pocket, sleeves and neck were decorated with what I knew as rickrack braid, a wavy contrasting band of colour.

Unknown to me Gary had arranged for Mary's mother, a much-respected elder and highly skilled seamstress, to make me a *quspuk* as a surprise. I didn't know it at the time, but Mary was shrewdly assessing my size at this meeting, in order to let her mother know my *quspuk* dimensions.

Both women were very attractive with long glossy dark hair tied up or back, and light olive smooth skin. They appeared Asiatic. Their eyes were small and almond shaped. They had short noses and beautiful smiles.

In front of each of their computer screens were framed tiny photos of family members – babies, children, teenagers, adults and elders – which they proudly showed me. Each photo seemed to have been taken by a school photographer using the same mottled deep-blue background.

'Oh, so you've met each other.' Gary walked out into the foyer. 'Come on in.' He was beaming proudly as he led me into his office.

Pictures of us both were on his desk. It felt strange seeing familiar faces there, like stepping onto the moon and finding your doormat from home lying there. The room was very dusty. The fine silt thrown up by the four-wheelers had seeped under the windows and doors, and covered everything like a fine talcum powder. Apparently winter was a much cleaner time of year.

There was a knock on the door.

'Come in,' Gary called out. 'That'll be James, my deputy,' he said. 'I told him to come and meet you.'

'Howdy ma'am,' said James. 'So pleased to meet you.' He grinned and ducked towards me, holding out his hand. We shook hands. James was a middle-aged man with a kindly smile. 'My wife, Susan, says to tell you y'all invited up to the house for dinner tomorrow night.' James and Susan had been in Tutalgaq for seven years. Susan taught in the elementary school. Their combined experience had been an invaluable source of information for Gary.

After James's visit, there was a constant stream of visitors to Gary's office; it seemed they all needed something from the principal. A chance to glimpse the principal's visitor perhaps? They all had demands. Students who had been in trouble were waiting in the foyer. I needed to go and let him get on with his work. Gary took me by the elbow and guided me back outside.

'I've just called Hageland Air,' he said quietly. 'I can arrange for you to fly to Mountain Village to meet the superintendent.'

'Oh great!' I was pleased. I needed to do this before I left.

'I've found a place for you to stay with Margaret, the district's reading specialist, and her husband. If you want you can leave Thursday.'

We smiled at each other. The first step of our plan had begun.

Chapter 8

Settling In

Three years earlier, when I left Sydney to return to New Zealand, I first flew to Christchurch, where my father had bought a car for me ready for the six-hour drive south to Balclutha. I needed a car for work. He had found a small white Mazda from a dealer in the city. I had brought the money from my recently sold Toyota to repay him. In the end I'd sold my Toyota to my ex husband, who had agreed to pick up the repayment contract I was on. I knew he would follow through. He needed a reliable car. This scheme was a win-win for both of us.

Dad insisted I wait till my first pay cheque before paying him back. 'No dear,' he said kindly. 'Pay us back later in small instalments. Keep the cash to help set up your flat, you'll need it.'

I wasn't used to such support. I preferred independence, but I was very grateful for the help. My personal things, as well as some of my furniture were being shipped over from Sydney. I would definitely need some other stuff in the interim. The cash would be very useful till my first pay cheque.

My parents were quite taken with Bel. My father went to a local thrift shop and bought an old wooden playpen, which he fashioned into a cage for her by inserting an opening door. Inside Bel could stay safe, and her usual jumping and bounding would be limited to a small area. That would be perfect for the next couple of months.

'Quiet is what she needs,' said my father.

After a few days staying with my parents, I headed down south. My little car was packed to the roof with all sorts of things. I had Bel and her supplies, sheets, towels and blankets, dog crate and pen, home baking and my luggage. It was good to be finally heading to my new home. I was hoping I would have time to relax. I wanted time to process all that had happened to me.

My first week in the little teacher's flat had me scurrying around the town looking for second hand shops and spare furniture. I set Bel up in her little run and headed out to explore. There was no furniture in the lounge, but the flat came with a kitchen table and chairs, a single bed and a dressing table. I had passed some interesting second hand shops in Milton on my way through. There was a great antique shop there as well. I hoped to be calling in there when I was more settled.

My teacher neighbours were all away for the summer holidays. They'd be back when the holidays ended in a couple of weeks. I could see little flower gardens, and curtains in their windows. I was looking forward to meeting everyone.

The flat had been left spotless. I had been told that a nun had been living in the flat before me. She had been asked to move out because a teacher was arriving. Teachers had priority in the flats. I felt very guilty about making a nun move out, so when she knocked on my door one day, I welcomed her in. She was very brusque and came straight to the point.

'I've come back to let you know that I'll be digging out that patch of potatoes I planted by the fence,' she declared without smiling. 'Round early February.'

I wasn't Roman Catholic, but I wanted to show her I was a worthy person. I felt guilty about having this older hard-working woman move out because of me.

'Would you like to come and have dinner with me on Saturday evening?' I asked politely. 'It's the least I can do after you having to move because of me.'

'Thank you,' she replied, still not smiling. 'I'll be here at 6 pm.' This first invitation was interpreted as a weekly one. I guessed she thought I was lonely. It became her duty to provide company for me on a Saturday night.

One Saturday after our evening dinner, I discovered that the sister was of the Mary MacKillop order of nuns, a sister of St Joseph of the Sacred Heart. I had brought some souvenirs from Mary MacKillop house in Sydney when I visited it in 1994. I kept them in my bedroom drawer along with my Maori bible.

Shortly after being introduced to the Maori community in Redfern in August 1994, I had been invited by elders to share in a special ceremony. They were removing Maori artefacts from storage in the bowels of the Sydney Museum. The items were being moved to MacKillop house in preparation for Pope John Paul II's visit early in 1995. He was to beatify Mary MacKillop as Australia's first saint. I learned that Mary MacKillop had spent much time in New Zealand with the Maori people. I also learned she had experienced much suffering. I remember at the time praying to her for a miracle, a way out of all my woes. Praying was something I had rarely ever done before.

I explained all this in reverential tones to the sister. I went and fetched the souvenirs to show her. I laid the cross and beads on her lap.

'Good,' she declared picking them up. 'I couldn't go to that ceremony, but now I have something from that special time.' With a nod and small smile she placed them in her pocket. 'God is kind.'

I didn't like to ask for them back. I thought the least I could do was let her have them. Anyway, my prayers had been answered. Look how things had worked out! Look where I was living now!

'It's the wairua, the spirit,' Paratai would say. 'It's just wairua, darling.'

Chapter 9
An Elementary School Visit

I had arranged to visit Tutalgaq's primary school situated at the bottom of the hill. Gary held the door open on the truck. 'The old village housing is down there, honey.' He climbed into the driver's seat and paused before placing the key in the ignition. 'Be prepared.'

The school was on the flat at the foot of the muddy trail that ran past our place and ended at the river. Gary had already warned me about what I would see. Raw sewage often spilled out onto the playground from broken pipes in the village. Although there was some old rotting wooden boardwalk so one could walk above it, kids often played down there on the ground. It was a major health hazard.

I had seen a lot in my teaching career. 'It doesn't worry me,' I said, smiling confidently at him. 'I'm sure I can manage.'

'Okaaaay,' he lilted back at me.

But by the time the truck had rocked its way to the bottom of the track, I had changed my mind. I had *never* seen anything like *this*.

The housing was decrepit. Rotting boards forming lean-tos no bigger than garden sheds stood in random clumps among the rubbish. Doorways had partly cured skins hanging nailed over them to keep out the cold. Worst was the rubbish and the smell that emanated from it. Old, broken-down snow machines with engines rusting lay where they had stopped; there were oil drums and rusted discarded pieces of machinery, household furniture and everything else imaginable. A rotting, putrid smell was in the air.

Mangy dogs prowled through the debris; short ropes tethered others to housing piles. There was howling and yapping. A lot of noise and no order to anything. Everything was caked in mud and dust. It was as if the huts were in a rubbish dump. I swallowed my shock. It was rude to stare.

'Come along,' Gary said cheerfully as he helped me out of the truck. I couldn't answer. I was silently trying to process what I saw. We carefully stepped over the rubbish that lay strewn on the ground as Gary guided me up onto the rotting boardwalk.

I knew I was seeing a culture that had undergone massive change. Potato chip and biscuit wrappers, and discarded cans of fizzy drink would not have lain here 50 years ago. The village wouldn't have existed either.

The Yup'ik Eskimo people had been naturally nomadic, following the herds for food. They had made temporary camps in the winter and settled longer at the summer fish camps. They had used the warmer months to gather and prepare their food for the long cold stretches of wintertime that lay ahead. They had utilised every part of the animal they hunted. They'd fashioned clothing, shelter, utensils and hand-made hunting implements. In contrast to what I was now seeing, nothing had been wasted.

I had read that when these parts were colonised, the colonisers had insisted on imposing their own education system. Villagers were forced by law to stay put, and children were ordered to attend school. So gradually over time the culture had started to erode as the traditional roles of hunting and gathering changed and weakened.

Gary took my hand as we picked our way along the boardwalk up to the elementary school doorway. Some small children were outside. One of them, braver than his friends, called out to us.

'Are you two honeys?' There was wild giggling at the bravery of that call from them all. Gary grinned.

'Yes, Travis. This is Emma. She is from New Zealand.'

A large cluster of older children ran over. Although they did not speak much, they were not shy. Some pulled at my top. They made personal comments.

'Twisty,' a girl said, touching my long hair.

'It's called curls.' I smiled.

'You speak funny,' another said. They were giggling at the strangeness of it all.

All the children looked small. Their clothing was dirty and some did not have shoes. Others had huge shoes that slopped up and down as they walked. Their hair was glossy and shiny. Their faces were serene. Their teeth were gapped or covered in black fillings.

Gary opened the main door into the school and led me to one of the classrooms. He opened the classroom door. Two *gussaq* teachers were seated there at a children's table, small plastic trays of hot food in front of them. One was James's wife Susan. I had visited her at home a few nights earlier.

Susan smiled at me as I stood in the doorway. I had given my boots a quick wipe on the doormat. I noticed the women were wearing indoor shoes. I hesitated. What was the protocol?

'Don't take your boots off, Emma,' she called to me. 'Too dirty for socks.'

'Take good care of her,' Gary said. 'I'll be back after school and pick her up.' He gave me a kiss on my cheek and left.

I stepped into the brightly decorated classroom. Susan introduced me to Heather, who was the kindergarten teacher. Heather's husband taught upper elementary school.

'I'll take you around later and introduce you to everyone,' Susan grinned. We got along well.

'Great, thanks,' I smiled, pulling up a chair near them. The women were eating school lunches. 'That tasty?' I asked. The food was on little plastic trays with compartments for different foods.

'Not bad for five dollars,' laughed Susan. These meals were planned to include each of the major food groups. I could see mashed potato made from flakes, some corned beef with a pasty white sauce and watery canned peas. The glass of milk on the side of the tray was made with powdered milk. It looked diluted. None of it looked appetising to me.

'Everyday the school cooks prepare a hot lunch for the children,' Susan explained. 'A breakfast of cereal and toast for them in the morning as well.'

'The students are classified below the poverty line,' Heather continued. 'So the meals cost them nothing. School is often the only place where children can get their food each day. The faculty can buy theirs at $5 a tray if they want. Most do.' Heather stood up. The bell was about to ring and the women quickly tidied up. 'It's a large saving in time and effort. Cheaper than shipping in your own supplies.' Heather took the trays and left to go back to her own classroom.

Susan went over to the sink.

'The children always clean their teeth when they arrive in the morning and again after lunch,' she explained. Lines of small toothbrushes were in stands there. This class was first grade. Susan took out a large tube of toothpaste and, walking around, began squeezing it out onto small, cut-up pieces of paper on each desk. 'With all the sugared drinks, dental decay is a huge problem out here.' I nodded in agreement. I had seen the children's teeth when I arrived.

As she chatted a handful of the very smallest children quietly walked in, staring at me. They each took a toothbrush and sat down at their desks. They wiped their brushes on the toothpaste and dutifully began to brush. All eyes were on the tall *gussaq* in their classroom.

Susan introduced me. 'Children, this is Emma,' she explained. 'I told you we were going to have a visitor. Emma has come all the way across the world, from New Zealand.' She walked over to a large map suspended over the board and pointed out the journey that I had taken across the world. The children followed with their eyes. They brushed and watched. No one spoke.

'*Waqaa,*' I said. Some grinned and bowed their heads in embarrassment. Others looked at each other and giggled. 'Pleased to meet you.' I continued, 'What good tooth cleaners you are!'

The children were eager now to show me just how good. The brushing began in real earnest. Some finished and stood up, moving to the sink to spit out the paste and hang up their brushes. They didn't take their eyes off me.

The children then moved to where Susan was sitting on a small rocking chair on a brightly patterned rug. Another small chair was beside her. The children sat down cross-legged on the rug. Her class obviously already knew the routine. They shot me little sidelong glances. For a junior elementary class, the room was so unusually quiet.

I sat down on the chair next to Susan and pulled out a little book I had brought with me about a kiwi in New Zealand. Leaning forward and smiling gently, I began to read.

Chapter 10

Locals and Distant Penpals

One morning in Balclutha, after the week school began, there was a knock at the door. Standing on my doorstep was the local principal and four older students. Everyone was carrying a piece of furniture.

'Morning Emma, I heard you could use these.' Mr Mark, the principal, laughed at the expression on my face as in walked chairs, a small desk and a sideboard. 'Oh . . . *thanks*.' I wanted to hug them.

'Let me know if you need anything else,' he said as they left.

My neighbours had all come home. Merv, who was retired, and his teaching wife Evelyn invited me over for dinner. Carol, an elementary teacher who had lived there seven years, had delivered a cake. I was starting to feel like I belonged.

During one of the visits to a local school I met a Maori kuia named Mona, who was the principal there. I had wanted to make contact with local Maori elders as soon as possible. It was correct tikanga, protocol. I took one look at Mona's classroom with a small group of country students huddled around a pot-bellied stove and I was reminded of my teaching inspiration, Sylvia Ashton-Warner, and her small country classroom with pot-bellied stove. Mona and I had an immediate affinity.

Mona told me over morning tea that she was starting a night class in te reo (Maori language) at the high school. I signed up and went along. The kuia and I soon became quite friendly. Each day I was feeling more and more at home.

One evening I was sitting at my little desk in my flat in Balcutha when I decided to take a break from study. Leena, a friend from Sydney, had sent me a web page address that she thought I should take a look at. Leena, who was part of a close group of Chinese friends and family, had been one of my Sydney friends who had worried about my sudden huge life change. She couldn't understand how I could live so estranged from all I knew in Australia and not even near relations in NZ.

Leena was very caring. As a GP to the Chinese community, she was a fount of useful remedies. When I had had the flu, on more than one occasion she had dropped off to me a pot of chicken soup with a sprinkling of Chinese herbs on her way to work. We were both single and had had a lot of fun together trying out some ballroom dancing lessons. We used to pull faces at each other over our partners' shoulders, giggling wildly at the bravery of daring to dance so closely in a stranger's arms. We often ate at each other's homes or local restaurants together. Our daughters were friends. Sometimes, in the quiet of Balclutha, I missed Leena's friendship. I was anxious to see her when I returned for Ella's birthday in July.

I looked at the web page. She had written, 'Emma, this'll be a fun way to meet more people, pen pals! Ella tells me all you do is work and study, study, study.'

The whole idea of pen pals bored me; it would just be more writing. Leena and I were similar, though. I wondered if she really wanted me to try this internet idea out for her. Maybe if it worked for me, she might be brave enough to try it.

This evening after a particularly long assignment, I decided to pull up the web page. It was offering a one-week free trial. So no commitments, nothing to lose.

It asked me to log in with a pseudonym. I thought a moment. 'Emzel' sounded good to me. Sort of like Emma in NZ. Next they wanted a personal email address. Apparently anything written to me could be forwarded through their filter. This filter protected both parties from sharing personal email addresses unless they chose to. With seven days free trial I had nothing to lose. I continued.

What country did I want? I ticked every country it offered. What religion? Same. Male or female? Male. What age group? Age groups were arranged in 20-year bands. I checked the one I was in. Pen pals or relationships? Both. I pushed 'Enter'.

My jaw dropped. Now I had a page that told me I had over 500 immediate matches! There they were marching down the page, arranged alphabetically according to where they lived; some even had small pictures. They came from all over the world. This was amazing. Here were all these men out there looking for someone. I never knew. I got up and made myself a hot chocolate, and hurried back to the computer. I prepared to settle and read.

Starting with the As on the first page I found Aceman, in Alabama. Aceman was an African American high-school teacher in Birmingham, Alabama. I sent him off a quick email. My ex had been African American, so Ella was also part African American. I felt an immediate affinity with Aceman.

'Hello Aceman,' I wrote. 'What is teaching like there in inner city Birmingham? I teach here in country New Zealand.'

I carried on skimming down the page. Alaska. The next was Alaskaman, someone working with indigenous people. How interesting. I had just come from working with the Aboriginal and Maori people in Australia. Close relationships with indigenous people had been a theme throughout my life. I shot off an email to Alaskaman.

I was starting to get bored now. I needed to get back to my study. I quickly skimmed on down the page till I got to Arctic, and read,

'Arctic NW. Kotzman. I live alone with my dog, am interested in other cultures.'

My goodness! NW Arctic. Alone with a dog. Interest in other cultures. I have found a polar opposite! Incredulous, I sent off a third email, this one to 'Kotzman in the Arctic Circle'.

Someone once asked me what I thought might have happened if I had started at Z instead. Would I be living in Zambia or Zimbabwe, perhaps?

I never did get out of the As.

Chapter 11

A Joke at Camp

Pilot Station school was undergoing a massive new building development. I had seen it from the air. The new school on a single site was to open the following fall of 2002. I could hear the hammers banging and machines rumbling all day on the hill up behind our house. Having visited the elementary school, I could understand the village excitement.

The construction company had flown in their own chef. On his arrival in early July, Gary had followed his nose to the wonderful smells of bacon cooking that drifted through our back door. He had since spent many a mealtime up there before my arrival. Twenty men on eight-week shifts took a lot of feeding. Well, 21 men.

The camp was definitely a 'man-zone'. Few if any women went there. 'The men are there to work long hours and make as much money as possible. They do much of the work under floodlights at night,' Gary had written. He had been fascinated.

I was not really keen on this visit. Gary had told me he had promised the construction site manager, Mike, he would introduce me. He had loaned Mike a spare mattress and in return he had been fed. Both men had become good friends. Mike was eager to meet this New Zealand woman. He wasn't sure he believed Gary's story of a woman coming all the way to Pilot Station from the other side of the world.

That evening we went up to the camp, the building site of the new school. The track was muddy and I was wearing my gumboots again. Gary had hold of my hand. Without warning my feet suddenly slid out from under me and I was face down in the muddy track. I was surprised at how fast it had happened. Apparently I had hit a small puddle that had frozen over. I hadn't hurt myself, but my confidence in walking on this rough and icy terrain had suffered a huge blow. Clutching Gary firmly, I walked much more slowly up the slope to camp. I would need to buy better boots for the coming winter.

Before I had arrived I had heard stories from Gary about the vehicles used in the school's construction. This sort of stuff impressed him. 'The vehicles are so large that the tyres are taller than my head,' he had written.

Once we got up to the site I could see what he had meant. The school that was being constructed would be two storeyed. The vehicles were huge. They were taller than the single buildings. These vehicles had been barged in over the summer.

'How on earth will they get them out?' I stood and stared in wonder at the enormity of the work vehicles.

'They'll stay until the next summer when most of the main building's construction will be finished. Then they'll barge 'em back out.' Gary squeezed my hand.

'Come on, honey.'

We entered the camp building. It was a series of connexes, like railway carriages, welded together to make one long metal hall. The flooring was formed from sheets of plywood. Doors led off this main corridor to more connexes placed at right angles, which were used as bunkrooms for the men. Lights were strung from the ceiling. Extension cords feeding the electricity were suspended in drifts above our heads.

In the centre was a long table. When we entered, the delicious smell of hot food enveloped us. Approximately 20 men dressed in work clothes were seated eating. The noise of their banter was loud, echoing down the metallic walls.

Mike stood up and beamed. He walked towards us, hand outstretched in greeting. 'Welcome! You must be Emma,' he said to me.

'Hi, Mike,' I nodded.

Gary had been telling the truth. His woman had arrived, and sounding by her accent, she was definitely not American. Our exchange seemed to transmit a secret message to the men. Immediately and silently they rose, almost in unison, and disappeared into their rooms.

Without comment, Mike took us up to the warming counter filled with hot food. It was like a walk-in buffet. I noticed Gary really piled up his plate. This was good American style eating. Huge steaks, mashed potatoes and gravy. Baked beans and cornbread. I couldn't see any vegetables anywhere.

Carrying a plate in one hand and orange juice in the other, we made our way back to the table. By now it had been completely vacated by the workers. I felt very relieved, but Mike looked annoyed. Gary just looked hungry.

The talk was short, but there was tension. I was pleased when Gary refused the coffee and dessert and we left.

The following morning Gary told me that Mike had rung him to apologise.

'Mike says the men have had a big telling off. He reckons they acted disrespectfully to us both.'

'What! Are you kidding?'

Gary shrugged and shook his head. I knew he agreed with me. He didn't look happy either. 'He says they should have remained at the table.'

'Of course they shouldn't have. I understood why they got up.' I had just been pleased that the visit was over.

Gary forced a reluctant smile. 'Mike insists we return, honey.'

'*Really?*'

'This time the men will join us.'

'You are not serious!' I searched his face, but there was no smile. With such a fuss made about it all, I could see I had no choice.

Two nights later, we headed up there again. This time we went by truck. I so badly wanted it over with. I felt like I was violating the men's personal space. This was not a restaurant, it was their work place.

When we walked through the door, the same vision of the previous visit greeted us. The smell was still overwhelmingly delicious, but something was wrong. Although 20 men were sitting there, the room was almost silent. Uncomfortably silent.

I could see hair damp and slicked behind the ears. Elbows were in. No swear words. They were on the boss's orders. A lady was visiting. They were to behave like gentlemen.

I was so embarrassed I fumbled my plate and nearly dropped it. Gary didn't seem to be fazed. His plate was piled high again. Mike looked pleased. He had arranged for us to be seated right in the middle of the long table. He sat opposite us.

As I sat down I racked my brain for something to break this uncomfortable silence. A joke. Any joke to break the ice, make people laugh and relieve the tension.

In the pressure of the moment I could think of only one joke. I launched straight into it without thinking.

'Did you hear the one about the two gay men playing party games?' I began. I immediately realised I had made a huge social faux pas. This was NOT a joke to share in this company, at this place. It was too late.

Mike looked at me and said, 'No.' He looked a bit surprised. I felt Gary's knee poke me in the thigh. Mike waited expectantly. Knife and fork poised. Should he take another mouthful? I couldn't take the words back. There was only one thing to do. Carry it off. I gulped. My mouth had gone dry. I started as brightly as I could.

'Well, they were playing, Guess the Vegetable.' I smiled stupidly and continued thinking, what an *idiot*! 'The first one picked up a carrot. "Feel this?" he said.

"Oh," his friend gasped, "that feels sharp and pointy . . . is it a carrot?"'

I could feel Gary's embarrassment next to me. His elbow was digging into me, and his knee was pressing into mine. Heat radiated from him. Still I went on. I really had no choice.

'Then he picked up a cauliflower and pushed. "Ooohhhh," said his friend, "that feels soft and round. Um . . . is it a . . . cauliflower?"' The room had become even more silent. More ears were listening to this than I wanted.

Mike had still not taken a mouthful. His food was balancing on the end of his fork. His mouth remained open.

'Then his friend picked up another vegetable . . . a root vegetable . . . um, white and pointy . . . um . . .' I pretended that I couldn't think of the word. Mike leaned forward in his chair. He wanted to help me out of this predicament. He raised his eyebrows.

'A parsnip?' he offered helpfully. I looked at him and waited. I made a deliberate pause.

'Oh,' I said looking at him with fake surprise, 'so you've played this game too?' Mike looked a little confused. By this stage Gary had his nose in his food. He was practically inhaling it off his plate. What was left of it.

Mike's face was blank.

Oh boy, I thought. Is he deeply offended? Maybe he's going to stand and tip over the table. For several full seconds there was a dead silence. We locked gazes. Then Mike blinked. Something had registered. He threw back his head and shouted with laughter. Slapping the table in time with his bellows he roared, 'Hahahahaha! Hahahahaha!'

Whew! The whole table burst into spontaneous raucous laughter too, either at the joke, or me, or Mike laughing loudly like that. I couldn't tell.

Mike thumped the table again. 'Love it! Tell Big Pete that joke. Go on. I dare you!'

There were heavy footsteps at the door and Big Pete, who had heard his name, thumped down to the centre of the table. He was about seven foot tall and covered with tattoos. Everyone shuffled along. There was screeching of metal on metal as Big Pete pulled out a chair opposite me.

'What joke?' Big Pete said in a deep bass voice. He looked at me steadily. The room had dropped to dead silence. The show was on. It was a silence heavy with promise. Promise of great enjoyment about to follow.

With a deep breath I again launched into the joke. It was the sort of joke that I would normally never tell. I had gay friends. The last thing I wanted was to offend anyone. The only reason I had remembered the stupid joke, was that someone had told it recently, and I remembered falling for it myself.

When I got to the punch line this time, Big Pete didn't drop his gaze.

'You don't think I'm going to fall for *that* one do you?' he roared. The table broke out in riotous laughter again. Big Pete already knew it! One up for the camp. But I was a star.

Mike pumped Gary's hand vigorously as we left. 'Come back *anytime*!' he called after us, chuckling. The men nodded. Some even stood as I passed by. They were grinning at me. This was more like it.

Gary led me firmly away by the elbow. His relief was apparent, but our departure seemed much more important to him.

'Well honey, you nailed it. We won't need to go back *there* again.'

Chapter 12

Poles Apart

I wrote again to Kotzman, 'I live in a small town on the south east coast of New Zealand, in the South Island. It faces into the wind that blows off the Antarctic. I live alone with *my* dog.'

'That's amazing!' he wrote back. 'I am in education, what do you do?'

'I am a resource teacher. I travel around schools offering support working with students and staff. What about you?'

'I am a high school principal.'

Kotzman wrote that he was living alone in the Arctic Circle, apart from his beloved golden retriever Mato. Unlike the emails I received from my other two pen pals, there was a strange inexplicable familiarity about this man. Our connection was different from the start.

'How come you are using this website?' I asked, after explaining how I had ended up there.

'It was my daughter's idea,' he explained. 'We were both living in Sitka, Alaska before I got this job. She was worried about me stuck up in the Arctic Circle all alone.'

His daughter had thought he needed a companion.

'She told me,' he wrote in his email, 'there's a really good website, Dad, you can go online without anyone knowing who you are,' Kotz explained. 'You just use a pseudonym.'

I chuckled to myself.

'I wasn't too sure about it,' he continued. 'But I thought I'd give it a go. I live in Kotzebue, in the Arctic Circle, so Kotzman sounded anonymous enough.'

Just like me, he had finally logged on in April 1999 on a one-week's free trial. It was the same week that I had logged on for mine.

The emails to Kotzman quickly grew into a daily routine. Through his emails I was learning what it was like to live in Kotzebue with the Inuit.

'I'm actually from the Mid West, Illinois,' Kotz wrote the following week. 'Corn and soybean country. I had been recommended to come to Alaska by a couple of professors I had been studying with.'

Kotz had then spent several years in Sitka, Alaska directing a secondary teacher preparation program at a college there. 'I reckon those professors knew what they were doing. I reckon they were looking for an excuse to visit someone in Alaska.'

He had been adding smiley faces over the last couple of days. This was a new trick he had recently learned from his daughter. He told me she had a son. Kotz was a grandfather. He had a granddaughter as well, his son's child. His son was living in Kodiak, Alaska. Commercial fishing.

'So what took you to Kotzebue?' I asked.

'The students did. I loved the teaching program and flying out to the bush to visit student teachers. So after seven years in Sitka, I decided to walk the talk. Go out there and do it myself. As well, the students I taught ended up earning more than me at the college,' he explained. 'About three times as much. I thought it was about time to make some money myself.'

Okay, so he had been struggling too. I understood money worries all too well.

'The prospect of working as a principal in the Arctic Circle excited me,' he wrote. 'I got a job through the April Job Fair for teachers in Anchorage.' Apparently this was a place where districts touted for customers. It lured people into the vast stretches of Alaska. The Alaska that lay in wait for the unwary, way beyond the city.

'Out of all the districts I looked at,' he continued, 'Kotzebue offered the best pay package and health benefits.'

'What sort of health benefits?' I asked. I hadn't heard of any school district offering health benefits before.

'Free dental and medical care. Those things can be really expensive out here. Kotzebue was also relatively easy to get in and out of. Jets land here.' Wow, jets. Fancy that, I thought. I was very surprised that jets actually landed in an Inuit village. There was another similarity between us. Ease of plane access had been important for Kotzman. Just like me when I had decided to come to Balclutha.

A couple of days later we emailed back and forth about education and the kids. I wrote and told him that I found the kids in South Otago were great country kids. Quite practical. Not many Maori though. From growing up in Whanganui I still remembered missing all the brown faces when my family first moved back to Christchurch. I had been in my second year of high school at the time.

'One hundred percent Inupiat here,' Kotz wrote. He had explained that Inupiat was the correct term for the people. Inuit was a collective term for a much larger group of people that included other native people.

'In my first days in Kotzebue, I was really shocked at the student's bad language. I heard it in corridors and classrooms everywhere.'

I was very surprised that swearing was a problem up there.

'It was a huge problem. I decided to hold a meeting with the parents and elders just after I started. I wanted them to watch some of the television programs their kids were watching. Would you believe they were getting their cultural information, impressions and vocabulary from programs you've probably heard of. Bevis and Butthead and MTV.'

Wow, I thought, they watch those programs up there? This ancient culture sure had some modern inroads into it.

'The thing was, the parents hadn't been watching. They were in for a shock when they did,' he continued. 'I had also spoken to the student council. Told them that people in the Lower 48 do not speak like that in everyday life.' Lower 48 was the term Kotz said everyone used to describe the rest of the contiguous United States. Apart from Hawaii, Alaska was the only other state not joined at the hip to the others.

'Having garnered the attention of the student council and supported by the parents and elders, the inappropriate language stopped immediately,' he concluded.

'Wow, that is amazing,' I wrote back. 'Did all the bad language stop that quickly?'

'Yes, it happened almost overnight. It was great. Fantastic people the Inupiat up here. They got it.'

Kotz said he loved that responsiveness and honest spontaneity, the trust that was placed in him.

'The student council accepted responsibility for bringing about the change and managed to minimise the inappropriate use of a routinely used expletive in two weeks!'

In response, I wrote descriptions of the rolling green South Otago countryside. I described Bel and my small apartment with its 'new' couch and two small rocking chairs I had bought for $40 from the second hand store in Milton. It was starting to look really cosy. I had bought a climbing yellow rose to grow up by my sunny kitchen window. It would look pretty in spring. Just as they did in Christchurch, roses thrived in this cold climate.

Kotzman told me he had had to look up where New Zealand was, as he wasn't quite sure of its position. 'I thought it was somewhere near Australia.'

That amused me. I knew from living in Australia how small New Zealand was to the rest of the world.

'Are there any igloos up there?' I asked Kotzman.

'Hunters build them when out on the ice, for survival purposes. Sorry to disappoint you, but everyone lives in cabins up here.'

Hmmm, interesting, I thought.

'I live in a rented apartment near the school. A drive up from the airport. It has a lounge, bathroom and kitchen. There is a flight of steps that lifts the apartment high above the blowing snows of winter.' He had described the gridded steel steps, from which the snow was now beginning to thaw in the light of the coming spring.

'It's getting brighter each day here,' he wrote a week later. 'We're heading into the long twilights of spring and summer.'

I knew about those. We had them in Balclutha too. I was surprised that there was actually a summer in the Arctic Circle. In my mind, I had only an imaginary picture of what his world looked like. I had imagined snow and ice, and blizzards constantly swirling. I imagined men braced against the strong winds, ducking in and out of igloos, gathering meat for the long winter months.

'We're gaining seven minutes a day of sunshine. Spring and summer fish camps aren't far away! Can't wait.'

Kotzman was going to go up the local river to a fish camp with Elmer, his Inupiat elder. He was taking a group of high school students for a two-week camp. Teaching them traditional values. They had done this for the first time the year before.

'It's absolutely amazing,' he wrote. 'The kids learn how to kill and dress a caribou. How to fish. The elders tell traditional stories around the fire at night. It's a chance for these kids to get away from the TV. Learn more about themselves.'

I knew they had TVs but it was still hard for me to imagine Inupiat sitting in rows watching TV up there.

'Tell me more about Elmer,' I wrote. Night classes in te reo Maori had started. I had been sharing stories about the Maori people and my Maori kuia.

Kotz responded with a long email about his experiences ice fishing with Elmer the previous winter.

'I had travelled with Elmer and his wife out to a special ice fishing place in the Kotzebue Sound,' he wrote. 'We went on snow machines way out. Elmer travelled on one pulling a sled. His wife also travelled on a snow machine, pulling a sled with two children on the back. I followed up at the rear. What amazed me was the white frozen landscape. It looked the same everywhere. Flat, with no points of reference, just like the cornfields of Illinois.

'Suddenly we stopped. In the middle of nowhere it seemed. This is what I wanted to see, I thought. The native way of making ice holes for fishing.

'Elmer walked around to his sled. He pulled off the tarpaulin. He picked up a six-foot petrol powered augur that was lying there. He swung it over to a spot on the ice. He hand-pulled the starter and the thing roared to life. In two minutes there was the hole! Elmer looked at my face and grinned at me, "We natives not stupid," he said. He moved over and made a few more holes.

'Elmer cut several holes in the ice, each about a foot, or as you'd say, 30 centimetres in diameter. The ice was about three feet or one metre thick. He then handed me a traditional ice-fishing line. Elmer's wife and kids had already chosen their own holes and were beginning to fish.'

Kotz had been watching them jig their lines up and down.

'The fishing pole he handed me was made out of two pieces of wood cut and fitted into a v shape. There was a string wound along the third side making a triangle. It was wound back and forth to secure it. There was a hook attached to the string. That hook was embedded into the wood for safety while travelling.

'When I took the rod,' Kotz wrote, 'I unravelled the string and dropped the hook as a lure into the hole. I squatted next to the hole like the others were doing. Elmer gave me a cup to scoop out the ice as it started to freeze back over.'

Elmer left Kotz to take up a fishing hole of his own. 'It wasn't long before I could see Elmer pulling fish after fish out of his hole. White sheefish. I still had not got a single bite!'

I could just imagine Kotzman sitting there watching and wondering, as a *gussaq* or white man, what was different about what he was doing.

'I jigged faster; I jigged slower, but still nothing. I could see the piles of fish growing alongside everyone else in the party, even the little kids were catching them. As the fish were pulled out of the holes they were freezing solid on the ice next to the catcher. What was I doing wrong?'

Elmer had stood up and walked over to where Kotzman was perched. Elmer nodded with his head. 'Here,' he said. Kotz stood where Elmer gestured, on the other side of the hole.

'I thought Elmer was teasing me. "Fish here," he said. Elmer watched as I dropped my line back in. On my very first jig I pulled up a white fish, my first sheefish. "Shadow," was all Elmer said in explanation.'

Chapter 13

Another Bush Flight

I was prepared for the flight to Mountain Village. This time I was not going to embarrass myself. I had been in bush Alaska over a week now and I was starting to feel more familiar with it all. I knew exactly what to do this time when flying. Don't ask stupid questions. Don't make inane comments. Just fly to Mountain Village as per Gary's instructions.

As soon as the call came over the VHF 'Plane landing in five', Gary drove me back up the short track to the airport in the school's ute. He didn't want anyone else to drop me off. He knew about bush flights and he was going to check that everything was okay. He hated the idea of me leaving even for this short trip. Gary went over the plans again with me.

'Now, honey, remember I have paid for your flight all the way to Mountain Village and back. You don't need to do anything.'

I nodded, listening intently.

'If there are any stops, remember you are booked all the way through. You are coming back tomorrow afternoon. Margaret said she would make sure you got your flight back.' I nodded.

We watched as the small plane suddenly appeared in the sky, circled the strip and skidded along the stones to our truck. The plane was bigger than the one I had arrived on. This was a six seater. The pilot opened his door and jumped down. Gary grabbed my overnight bag and strode over to the plane.

'Hi there, this is Emma. She's from New Zealand.' He was proud of that fact. New Zealand was a long way away. 'She's off to Mountain Village for a day or so.'

The pilot, a man I had never seen in my life before, turned to me and grinned. With a voice that was meant to mimic my Kiwi accent he said, 'Look at all the huts down there!' We all laughed, me with bright red cheeks. I was learning that, just as in small village gossip grapevines, amongst bush pilots word flies around.

Still chuckling to himself, the pilot opened a flap on the side of the nose of the plane and pushed my bag in. Opening the back door he pulled out some steps. With a small wave to Gary I clambered aboard. Even at this more temperate time of year, everyone was wearing heavy jackets, boots, hats and gloves. Gary had explained the need for me to dress so warmly. No one took any chances with extremely variable weather and the possibility that if the plane ditched or landed unexpectedly those aboard could die of exposure. A sobering thought.

A huge cargo net covered boxes, bags and all sorts of shapes. I moved forward and sat down on one of the little collapsible seats. I buckled myself in. No one took any notice of me at all. This time there were women on board, as well as men. Apart from me, all were native.

No voice recording here. Just pilot in, plane start, and go. We roared along the stony strip, soaring off the end of the cliff for the much needed uplift on this heavier plane. From my window I could see Pilot Station and Gary quickly diminishing from view. Once more I was suspended above the wilderness.

Gary's words came back to me. 'You'll be fine. I have booked you all the way through. There and back.' I knew that Margaret was looking forward to meeting a Kiwi teacher. 'They'll love you! See you tomorrow, babe!'

I was amazed at how quickly civilisation as I had begun to know it disappeared from view. I could see only a small stain in the bush that was Pilot Station. Wilderness stretched out forever in every direction.

I looked out again on vast and seemingly never-ending stretches of green, brown and silver. When I was down in the village, civilisation seemed close and ordinary, but within a minute of leaving I could see just how inconsequential our little settlement was. It was swallowed up in this vast land of endless bush and tundra.

We banked and droned our way forward. I kept my eyes on the riverbeds, trying to take in all that I could see. I was looking for moose now as well as bears. The noise became mesmerising. I put in the earplugs Gary had given me. He had told me that many became deaf through listening to these high decibel levels while flying.

Suddenly I heard the plane's engines changing. Were we stalling? Bush was still everywhere below, no sign of settlements. I knew accidents were common. The school district life insurance for flying was only a few thousand dollars. You flew at your own risk.

I looked at the other passengers. Someone had told me that when flying, 'You only start to worry when you see native women crossing themselves.'

No one was moving or looking anxious, so I swallowed my fear. As the plane suddenly banked steeply, I saw dwellings; I was not going to call them huts again. We circled, dropping suddenly. Next we were skidding very quickly along the airstrip. The plane pulled up outside a small building that looked familiar. St Mary's.

The pilot opened his door, and came around the back. He pulled down the steps. Passengers unclasped their belts and stood up. I knew what to do this time. While other passengers stood and doubled forward making their way back down the aisle and down the steps, I stayed put. They must all have been going to St Mary's.

The last passenger paused as he passed me. Raising his eyebrows and gesturing with his head to the door, he spoke quietly. 'You getting off?'

I shook my head and smiled. 'No, I'm going to Mountain Village.'

'This plane not.'

Chapter 14

A Letter from Joy

'Hello Emma, how lovely to hear from you.' Joy Cowley had written back to me, four days after I sent her my letter. I could not believe it. It had been a dream of mine to make contact with this New Zealand author. The author whose books I had used so successfully over the years with my students.

I had written to Joy the day I put the final full stop on my masters paper. Ten minutes later, after I had made myself a cup of tea, I had sat down with pen and paper and begun.

'Dear Joy, I know this is a bit cheeky of me to write to you, as you must get hundreds of letters all the time. I expect you're awfully busy as well.' I had written to her as if to an old friend. She had felt to me like an old friend. 'I'm writing as you are the treat I promised myself when I put the last full stop on my master's paper.

'While I was teaching in Australia, I used your stories with all my reluctant readers. Your words seemed to capture their hearts and minds. The kids loved them.' It had made me proud to be a Kiwi too.

I went on to tell Joy of my life in Balclutha and my recently finished studies. I told her I was planning on visiting Alaska. Then I got to the real point of my letter. 'I have these children's stories,' I continued. I could just imagine her inner groan, as she thought, Not another one! But I blithely carried on. 'I'm a bit of a storyteller myself. I used to tell my own stories to the children in my class in

Sydney. Sort of as a reward. The kids loved them, probably more as a break from schoolwork than for any other reason.' The stories did the trick though. There was always total enthralled silence throughout my recounting.

'The stories were all based on my own childhood experiences. The naughty and silly things I did growing up in Whanganui. One of the parents urged me to write them down.' The kids used to sit and read the stories over and over again in their spare time. 'Another parent, an artist, encouraged me to send them off to a big Australian publisher.' I still remembered that vividly. I had been flattered by her suggestion. 'Anyway, the upshot was that I got a letter back from the publisher a month later. She was excited by the stories and had sent them to one of the editors in her company. He was also keen. The question was, 'Would I rewrite them set in an Australian context?'

Even though everyone was very excited for me, I just couldn't do it. I couldn't set my childhood in Australia. I had grown up in Whanganui, for goodness sake! So the stories had languished for years in my drawer.

I had shared the story-writing saga with Kotzman. 'Why don't you look for a NZ publisher now you are home again?' he had asked.

So I had decided to ask for Joy's advice. Now four days after mailing my letter, here was her response.

'I was so interested to read your lovely letter,' Joy wrote. She gave me some very useful advice on publishing options, particularly for children's stories. I would do that when I got a chance. Then she went on, 'Do you know I have actually visited bush Alaska five times?' No, I had had no idea at all. 'If you're not faint-hearted you should try *akutaq* – Eskimo ice cream,' she continued. 'It is made of whipped reindeer tallow, seal oil and blueberries.'

Joy told me she had listened for hours to the stories told by the Alaskan elders. But the stories had been told in English. She had wondered how much more meaningful these stories would have been in their own language.

Her letter finished, 'Please do keep in touch.'

I was thrilled. I would.

Chapter 15

St Mary's Again

'I need to talk to the principal at Pilot Station!' I could hear my panicky voice cutting through the quiet room. I was standing at the counter at St Mary's. I had to get to Mountain Village. Gary told me he had paid the ticket from Pilot Station to Mountain Village and back. The other passengers had disappeared and the room was empty.

The bored native counter attendant, obviously used to flying *gussaqs*, said again slowly, 'Sorry. No more planes in or out today.'

'Can you please call Pilot Station?' They passed me the phone. Gary was on the line. 'I'm in St Mary's. No more planes today.' I tried to keep the fear out of my voice.

'What? Let me speak to someone!'

I could hear the attendant saying it again. 'Sorry, not enough passengers for more flights today. Sorry.'

I turned to another woman behind the counter who was listening in. 'What can I do? I have people waiting for me at Mountain Village.'

'Sleep here on floor. Plane fly tomorrow.' She was trying to be helpful.

'But I have a big appointment in Mountain Village tomorrow!' I was getting a rapid lesson on the dangers of flying in the bush. Do not count on anything. Weather, seats or bookings. Planes fly when and where they want.

Amidst all the kerfuffle a small man in a black leather jacket appeared from behind the counter. He was a *gussaq*. 'Are you Emma Stevens?' he asked.

'Yes.' I was about to burst into tears. Someone naming me here immediately made me feel less lost.

'Oh,' he laughed. 'You're in luck. You're coming to *my* place tonight.' It was Tom, the reading specialist's husband. Apparently he was an aircraft technician and he worked here in St Mary's. I was saved.

Well . . . maybe. Tom looked me up and down.

'Have you got any more warm clothing?'

'Yes, I have another vest in my bag.'

'Well, put it on, you're going to need it.' He nodded perfunctorily. 'Gloves, scarf and hat too.'

'Oh?'

Tom smiled reassuringly. 'You can ride home with me on the back of the four- wheeler.'

Tom took the phone and explained his plan to Gary. Gary wanted to check I was okay with the arrangement. Tom passed me the phone.

'Honey, are you okay with travelling on the four-wheeler?' He sounded worried.

'Yeah, I'm good.' I spoke with more confidence than I was feeling. What were my alternatives?

'Well, you'll need to rug up well. Call me when you get there, okay?'

'Yeah, don't worry, I will.' I hung up. Tom arrived from around the back on a red quad bike. I gulped. It looked pretty small to fight off bears.

I passed Tom my bag, and he strapped it onto the carrier at the back. He then sat back on the machine. I stepped onto the foot-rest and slung my leg over the back. This was great. It was like riding the motorbikes I had enjoyed in my teens. Tom revved the accelerator and we set off out across the tundra. I put my hands each side on the rack behind me and gripped for balance.

Instead of taking the 22-mile journey down a trail that reached between St Mary's and our destination, Mountain Village, we headed straight out across the tundra. 'I know a short cut,' Tom yelled over his shoulder.

The journey was so strange. No trees here, just soft spongy ground with small lakes, swampy tussock and gravel embedded in dark peat-like soil. Tundra.

We bumped and slid along. I used every muscle in my buttocks to cling to the seat without grabbling hold of Tom. That would be too embarrassing. I was a Kiwi woman, after all. I could ride on the back of a four-wheeler without clinging to any man.

I could not believe that in such a short space of time, I was now sitting on the back of a four-wheeler behind a complete stranger, in the middle of an alien and dangerous landscape, and trusting him with my life.

The journey reminded me of a news clip I had seen of astronauts on a moon buggy. Over every horizon, there was yet another gentle undulation. With no bushes or signs of any vegetation over ankle height, it felt like we were riding over the horizon's edge into infinity. The sun was getting low, and it was becoming severely cold. I ducked my head down behind Tom's back to break the freezing air. The tyres were sinking slightly into the soft ground.

On and on and on we went. I wondered what my family would think if they could see me now.

My father had been gloomy when I left New Zealand. He didn't think I should travel so soon after 9/11. 'The second world war started after an attack on Pearl Harbour,' he warned. 'Your mother and I think you are *crazy* travelling all that way right now. Especially through the States. We wish you wouldn't go. Even if you get there, you may never get back again!'

I knew it was really much more his worry than my mother's. However, combining both of them in his statement gave it more seriousness, more weight. I wondered what they would think if they could see me now. 'What on *earth* are you doing?' they would say. The four-wheeler ploughed on and on and on.

We came into Mountain Village the back way. Margaret stepped out when she heard the four-wheeler pull up to her apartment. 'Great, you made it!' she grinned. 'I got a call from Pilot Station!'

Standing up, I definitely felt a bit stiff. Tom took my bag and we entered their warm and cosy house.

There seemed something special about making a house into a home in the bush. *Gussaq* houses seemed made of up dreams of a home elsewhere. Often the knick-knacks appeared quite incongruous with the surroundings. Lighthouses, farm scenes, plastic flowers and ivy were popular. Reminders of what was not naturally here. I had also seen much handwork, quilting and embroidery.

Most *gussaq* houses also displayed local native art and craft. There were baskets, beadwork, ivory and carvings. *Gussaq* teachers' money invigorated the local cash economy. The white people who came out were often here for a set amount of time and for a particular reason. Just like Gary. As he put it, 'We are either missionaries, mercenaries or models.'

Margaret had cooked us a pasta dinner. 'Pasta's easy,' she chatted. 'You just need dry noodles and tinned tomatoes. It's the salad and the glass of wine over dinner that we miss!'

Mountain Village had a population of around 800. Like Tutalgaq it was a dry village. Alcohol was a persistent problem in Alaskan village communities; so much so that a law had been introduced many years earlier to allow communities to decide on their own alcohol regulation. The villages could be of three types: wet, damp or dry. 'Wet' meant alcohol could be purchased in the village or brought in and drunk freely. 'Damp' meant you could bring it in yourself for your own consumption, no sales anywhere in the village. A 'dry' village meant no alcohol was allowed at all – there was a total ban on bringing it in or consuming it.

Most Alaskan villages were dry, but bootlegging was prolific. Alaskan State Troopers were always being called in to handle alcohol misdemeanours. Alcohol had wrought havoc with native culture. The fallout was seen everywhere: foetal alcohol syndrome, suicide, domestic violence and sexual abuse. It was true that many native peoples were not able to handle even one glass of wine. If you were caught with alcohol it could mean exile from the village, or even jail.

We chatted on into the evening, sipping our juice.

Chapter 16

Email Confessions

Balclutha evenings were getting cooler, and shorter. I now spent most of my time working and studying. Often on a Friday night I would walk Bel as far as her little legs would carry her, down at Kaka Point on the beach. Then we would sit on the sand. I would lean against one of the largest logs washed ashore there and eat hot fish and chips straight out of the wrapping paper. Bel would lick her lips in anticipation of the small pieces of fish I would save for her.

The sunsets here were spectacular. The New Zealand skies reminded me of the paua pieces I would gather on my walks. I needed now to be rugged up in jacket and gloves, as the evenings were drawing in and the winds could be quite cold. I thrived in this cooler weather. I could breathe deeply, and felt fresh and revived.

Often I would sing the Maori waiata I had learned in Sydney. The words would be snatched by the sea breeze as I walked the beach at sunset. I would think about my life.

I liked to come home in the darkening evenings, rake up the fire, log on and get an email about Kotz's day.

Kotzman and I were beginning to share more of our personal life history. I learned of his past hurtful experiences too. How he lost all his savings in a relationship that had gone bad, even all his retirement funds. It was comforting and cathartic to be able to share deep pain. I discovered a technique that helped me share difficult memories with him. I had been talking about my marriage break up. I would write what had happened, cover my eyes, and then push 'send'.

'It was so unfair,' I wrote. 'We had come to Sydney filled with hope and optimism for my husband's career, producing music. He sent out over 500 CVs outlining all his previous successful international experience as a guitarist with gold and platinum records, and his success as a record producer, including a recent number one hit in Japan, but the CVs had his photo in them. What interest was there? None whatsoever. He ended up having to wait tables!'

I had felt so sorry for him. We had wondered if the photo had actually been the culprit. Although he was African American with a Danish father, he looked Aboriginal in the underexposed pic, very much darker than he actually was. At that time racism against Aborigines in Sydney had been palpable. Having lived in a mixed marriage in Los Angeles in the late seventies, and New Zealand in the eighties, I had become hypersensitive to the social nuances that surrounded us. The racist experiences that we had shared over the years. We had both been subjected to racist comments, looks and attitudes on a daily basis. The music scene in Sydney seemed to favour white rock culture, which was not what we had expected. This preference appeared parochial and deeply rooted.

I had been forced to go back to work as our savings melted away. I had immediately been offered teaching positions. Then I won a Sydney prize for my teaching skills. I wasn't even supposed to be working; we had planned on home-schooling Ella. In the end it was me that had all the success. That had been another huge blow to my husband's self esteem. His hopes for a successful music career as a producer based in Australia just trickled away.

I blamed Australian societal mores for our marriage split up. No wonder I had wanted to go back to New Zealand. Dealing with our break-up had been very difficult.

'You know what I did?' I wrote to Kotz one day. 'I put on the Walkman, and started walking. I walked so far away from home I wasn't sure exactly where I was. I had no money.' I had been trying to walk out the pain.

'OK,' he wrote.

'So I sat down on the grass in a corner of a park and wept.'

I looked through my fingers. No comment from Kotzman. 'An Aboriginal bag lady came over and shook her bag at me. There was a strong smell of alcohol,' I went on. It felt cathartic to share this terrible day. 'I patted the grass and she sat down next to me. I let her put her arm around me.'

'OK,' wrote Kotzman. He's thinking I'm weird, but I needed to write. 'I felt so alone. Even though she smelt a bit, her warmth felt good. She seemed to know that.' Kotz is miles away, I reminded myself. In the North Pole. He'll never meet me.

I checked through my fingers.

'OK.'

He was still there. I forced myself to go on.

'I must've stayed there a couple of hours. She kept swigging and offering me some, but I didn't have anything to drink.' All I had wanted was her warmth. I continued, 'In the end I got up and took off my good jacket. Put it around her. Then somehow I found my way home. Got back about 10 pm. Really stupid thing to do.' Ella had been worried.

'No, not stupid.' Kotz wrote, 'You must have needed that.' Yeah, I had actually. I was glad he didn't lecture me.

'I don't think the bag lady even knew I'd left in the end.'

This writing was cathartic and liberating. I was telling Kotz things I would never have dared tell anyone else face to face. He was so far away it gave me space to do so. He had great empathy and he didn't judge me. It felt very good.

My other two pen pals were writing as well, but not as frequently and their emails did not have as much depth and detail as Kotzman's. During the initial first week of contact we had all dropped off the filter system that we had first logged onto and were now writing directly to each other.

'I teach high school drama,' wrote Aceman. 'I sometimes fly to New York at break times. I love the shows that are on there in that city.' We had an affinity in music – soul, and rhythm and blues. I had experienced some exciting times watching my ex recording in London and accompanying him to the Grammy awards in LA. His life as a successful musician had been exciting. Aceman and I had lots to talk about there.

My Alaskaman contact was more circumspect in his writing. I suspected he was writing to many others and had had lots of practice at it. I didn't get much personal information about him; he dodged personal questions. He often forwarded attachments from others that, as he put it, he had 'cleaned up' by removing all the forwarding details from the headings and subject lines. Alaskaman sounded lonely. I guessed Alaska could be a lonely place.

Kotzman's emails, as a contrast, were full of interesting information. 'Last year, in midwinter, I chaperoned the basketball team to Hawaii over the Christmas break,' Kotzman wrote one night. 'All the other faculty members were heading back to the Lower 48 for their Christmas.' I still had a hard time picturing Christmas in midwinter. 'The kids and I had a great time. They said they liked to leave Doc on the beach reading. Little did they know I was watching what they were doing from beneath my book.'

'Doc?' I asked.

'Yeah, that's the name the kids here call me.'

'Why Doc?' The expression reminded me of an old Elmer Fudd and Bugs Bunny comic strip, named after Bugs' famous line, 'What's up, doc?'

'I gave them a choice when I arrived at the school. You can either call me Mister or Doctor. The basketball team chose Doc and it stuck.'

I stared at the words.

'Doctor?'

'Yes. Didn't I tell you I have a doctorate in education?'

'No, you didn't.' I thought of all my emotional outpourings to him over these weeks. The blurting out. All the diatribes about myself. This was not the wild Alaska man of my imagination. This was an academic. How could I have forgotten? I logged off.

I knew Kotz would be wondering what had happened. Sometimes in the computer dial up I was using, the line would drop off. I could pretend that had happened here. I needed time to think.

This emailing had been a world away from the long pedantically academic essays I'd had to write for my studies, where I'd been very careful about grammatical correctness, which full stop went where when quoting from a source, and so on. 'Use the correct APA referencing style, please,' they'd kept reminding me, and I'd had to purchase a book on academic styles that had been recommended to me on more than one occasion by my lecturers.

Now here I was again. Kotzman was an academic. My dream world had bumped into reality. The last thing I needed or wanted was more pressure from an academic. I looked back over his writing. No mistakes. Oh no!

'Where are you, Sunshine?' He had started calling me Sunshine because he said Christmas in the sunshine stuck in his mind. 'Are you okay?' This man was an academic, a doctor! I felt terribly disappointed. Any fantasy I had had was in ruins. I was embarrassed now at my wild and spontaneous writing filled with mistakes. I sent him an email asking him to come back on line that night.

'As you know I am busy writing all these academic papers all the time,' I began later on that night. 'I have to be so particular with the sentence structure and grammar.'

'Yes, I know.' He sounded a bit short. A bit hurt. He usually wrote much more than this. And he would have called me Sunshine by now.

I took a breath and wrote, 'You know, I was a bit stunned when you told me you had a doctorate in education.'

'Yep, sorry.'

'I'm actually a really good speller.' How pathetic it looked out there in writing. 'I was really enjoying myself sharing my deepest thoughts with you. I wasn't paying any attention to my sentence structure.'

'That's okay with me.' He sounded like he wanted me to get to the real point.

'Well, when you told me you had a doctorate, I looked back over your emails and there isn't one mistake in them, not even a spelling mistake!' I could feel my ears red-hot.

'No,' Kotz wrote. 'That's because I used spell check.'

Spell check! Of course! I hadn't thought of that. He *had* made mistakes in his emails, but had just used the spelling checking tool before sending. Kotzman wasn't some kind of academic genius. This was more like it. I felt warm with pleasure at the relief of it all.

'Sunshine, are you OK?'

'Yes, fine.' We carried on as if nothing had ever happened.

I had not yet shared with anyone the fact that I was in email communication with a man. I knew it was becoming addictive, so I decided to talk about it and gauge the reaction from some of my new and closest friends in Balclutha, my teacher neighbours. Carol, Merv and Evelyn often shared meals with me on a Sunday night. We enjoyed each other's company. We took turns at each other's homes. Merv and

Evelyn looked after Bel for me if I had to travel to Dunedin overnight for my training. One evening over dinner, I casually mentioned my emailing.

'Um, I've been writing to someone on the internet.'

'Oh, have you?' Evelyn replied, as she placed the delicious smelling casserole on the table, and returned to the kitchen. 'Anyone interesting?' She took a sip of wine from her glass. I was thinking how to respond.

Without waiting for my response she continued, 'You know what?' She paused. 'We are thinking of looking for a house bus to modify for some travelling.'

Merv turned away from the sound system he had been fiddling with. He liked to get the music sound just right. He was a bit of an electronics guru. He grinned at me.

'Yeah, and guess who will come up with the plans, and who will do all the hard work?' Merv and Evelyn exchanged a smile with each other. They were very comfortable in each other's company.

It was obvious to me that the house bus was much more interesting than any emailing I was up to. I smiled at them in relief.

Chapter 17

A Visit to District Office

In the morning it was still dark when Margaret and I walked to the Mountain Village District Office. The two storeyed building shone out across the settlement and lit up our path as we walked the short distance from her home. Chicken mesh was stapled over all wooden walking surfaces. It would be easy to slip here when temperatures hit freezing point. Dozens of four-wheelers were lined up outside the office.

I was nervous. I needed to impress this superintendent. I badly wanted a job now. If I told him all I had been doing in Australia and New Zealand, maybe I could swing a job offer.

We started at the brightly lit reception area downstairs, where a native woman smiled at us from behind the counter. When Margaret introduced me I reached out my hand and nodded. '*Waqaa*,' I greeted her.

The woman grinned and nodded back at me. '*Waqaa* to you too.' As Margaret hurried me along, the woman and I exchanged a smile.

People walked in and out of the several offices as Margaret introduced me. This district office seemed to be filled with American *gussaqs*, all holding polystyrene cups of coffee in one hand.

'Howdy there!'

'Great to meet you!'

'I worked with Gary once, great guy!' And so on.

Suddenly a voice called out from one of the offices. 'Is that a Kiwi accent I can hear?'

I was impressed. Usually people thought me Australian.

'Yes, it is!' I called back in the same direction.

A tall man appeared at the doorway. 'Kia ora, I'm Jim Cresswell and welcome to Mountain Village,' he said. 'I have a good Kiwi friend who came here once. You might have heard of her – Joy Cowley. She's a writer.'

We stood and chatted a while.

Margaret called out. 'Going on up to my desk to check my emails. Come up when you've finished visiting.'

By the time I walked up to her office she'd had some disappointing news. The superintendent had been called out to one of the village schools. He wasn't in today.

'Don't worry,' she reassured me, looking at my disappointed face. 'His associate is in. We can go down and visit him later on.'

During my introductions around the office I had seen one door that hadn't been opened to me. Something told me I needed to go there alone. I asked Margaret if I could go for a wander.

'Yeah, sure. Come back when you get bored.'

I made my way back downstairs to that door. I knocked on it quietly. A native woman's voice responded in affirmation.

'*Ii-i?*'

I opened the door. The room was small, very small – almost the size of a broom closet. The woman was sitting at a computer. There was a chair by the door. As I entered she turned to greet me. She didn't seem surprised to see me.

'*Waqaa*,' she spoke quietly.

'*Waqaa*,' I replied. 'Can I sit?'

She nodded at the spare chair by the wall.

I introduced myself and told her where I had come from. She knew Gary. The woman told me she was the district's media specialist. I was still trying to figure out why I had felt I should be in here. The feeling was still very strong.

'I send resources to village schools,' she smiled. 'I taught geography before.' As she spoke, I realised why I had come in here. I knew now I needed to sing for her.

This had happened to me before. I could not explain it. Maori had been the most comfortable with it.

'It is the wairua, the spirit, Emma,' Paratai had said. 'It's tapu, sacred. Don't question it. Let it happen. It's a gift.'

I felt embarrassed. This was the last place I had expected or wanted this to happen. I was meant to be impressing people, not scaring them off. However I knew there was no use trying to suppress the feeling, as it would only become stronger.

'Excuse me,' I began tentatively. 'But is it okay if I sing for you?' She swivelled on her chair to face me. Her hands were in her lap. She showed absolutely no surprise at all. She nodded her head. I stood. Placing my heel hard against the door to keep anyone from coming in, I quietly prayed my voice would be soft. I didn't always have control over that.

'I will sing to you in Maori,' I explained. She nodded. The song would come. I never knew what it would be. Somehow it always came. We both waited in the silent room. Seconds passed and I began to sing. My voice was soft and low.

'E pa to hau, he wini raro, he homai aroha.' As the words washed over her, she began to weep quietly. *'He tangi atu au, i konei, he aroha ki te iwi.'* It was as if I were watching from a great distance, through a mist that lay between us. *'Ka momotu ki tawhiti . . .'*

The ancient waiata continued. I knew the words were of loss and memories. The room was charged with electricity. As I finished she reached out to me. We drew together in a long embrace. Through her sobs, she whispered in my ear.

'You knew, didn't you?'

'I only knew I had to come in here. To come in here, and then to sing.'

'You knew,' she whispered. 'You knew that my sister committed suicide last month.'

I was shocked. Quietly I told her the meaning of the words I had sung: 'The wind blows, bringing loving memories to me. I cry for those I have lost to the spirit world.'

Now we were both crying. She didn't want to let me go. We continued to hug. 'You come all the way across the world. You bring this message to me. It helps my family and me too. *Quyana* so much!' She was so filled with thanks that she didn't want to let me go.

Eventually I left her room. We had exchanged email addresses. She wrote to me later about the joy and hope my song had given her and her family.

Wobbly, I returned to Margaret. The spirit of wairua was still strong, so I had given myself a quick sprinkle of water from a tap in the bathroom on the way back. I was not about to share something so sacred that had happened. I knew that whatever had transpired had been for us only. Anyway, I didn't want to shatter Margaret's illusion of me as an eminently suitable employee.

I put my coffee down on her desk. Margaret was busy checking emails. She looked up at me. 'Having fun?' I nodded and turned quickly to look at the books on her shelves. I didn't want her to see that I'd been crying.

When she finished up the job at her desk, she took me downstairs. She introduced me to the associate superintendent and his wife, who was the curriculum coordinator. Both were friendly, and Margaret left me in their care. I spent the rest of my time at district office sorting out piles of curriculum documents. The bundles of documents were being sent out to the district's schools with directions for implementation.

Except for the elusive superintendent, I had now met everyone.

Chapter 18

Snow in Balclutha

Balclutha was heading into winter. It was becoming cold with frost and ice. Mid June we even had a snowfall. The schools that relied on bus transport were closed. Kotzman couldn't believe it.

'How much snow?' He asked me.

'Ten centimetres. That's four inches to you.'

'And they shut the school?' He was incredulous.

'Yes, the kids are coming in from the country. Roads can be treacherous, slippery.' I felt a bit silly describing snow to him when he lived in the Arctic Circle.

'You know up here if we get eight feet of snow, school is still on.'

'Eight feet! That's nearly two-and-a-half metres! We'd never be at school with your rules.' He went on.

'The only time we close the school is if I stand on my back porch and hold my thumb out. If I can't see it, it's too dangerous to travel, so I put a call out, "Snow day! School is shut".' Hmmm, that made me feel embarrassed.

'You know,' he wrote, 'teachers here don't ever want a day off.'

Don't want a day off, they must be nuts! I thought. Who wouldn't want a warm day by the fire instead of travelling to school in cold snowy conditions?

'Even in blizzards and with minus 50 degree temperatures teachers want to come. It's simple.'

'How is it simple?' I wrote.

'Any time school is shut for snow up here, it has to be made up in the summer months or on a Saturday. Summer means getting out to the fish camps, or heading home for summer if you're a *gussaq*. Going home to your family in the Lower 48. Saturday school is unpopular. It encroaches on the "my weekend time off" thinking. Students as well as faculty all think the same.'

I had been writing to Kotzman about a recent visit to a marae in Dunedin as part of my resource teacher training. I'd been away a week. Maori culture was an important part of the agenda. With my Maori experiences growing up in Whanganui and recent deep involvement with Maori in Sydney, I had a definite head start. I had been in my element.

'We had a hangi during our stay,' I wrote. 'Absolutely delicious. The meat and vegetables are cooked in the ground. Steamed on very hot rocks in baskets together. The wild pork was delicious too. It dripped through the flax basket and on to my fingers.'

'Don't talk about pork,' wrote Kotzman, 'my mouth is watering. We eat lots of fish and caribou up here. I have to say I am really enjoying seal oil though. There's a lot of seal oil up here. We get it from the hunting. It comes in three grades, fine, medium and heavy duty. Something like car oil. I really like medium best. It is used like salt. All food is dipped in bowls of seal oil before eating.'

Kotzman was preparing to head off to summer camp. School was nearly finished for the long summer break. Elmer and he had set up a culture camp the year before with the help of other elders in the village. Elders visited at different times to share their skills.

'You know this camp was a first time experiment last year. It was something the local Inupiaq elders had wanted for a long time.' I was intrigued.

'I worked out that the kids can gain credit for their studies. They have to attend for ten days in their summer holidays.' That sounded like an excellent idea. A way to reconnect with their culture, make learning authentic and meaningful.

'Many students had been failing through low attendance. This gave them a chance to pick up much needed credit.' Kotz sounded proud of this scheme. 'You know I was excited about the chance to include culture in a more meaningful way, and to work closely with the local elders. Amazing people.'

Over the next few weeks Kotzman wrote when he could. We had decided to try to keep in touch over his summer holidays. He would still be calling in to school periodically, so he could use the computer. He and Elmer had set up a tent camp north of Kotzebue on a long gravel spit. Kotz had taken his golden retriever Mato along.

Migrating caribou made their way past the camp on the way to calving grounds at that time of the year. The students were taught to butcher caribou as well as seal. They had set a gillnet arching into the sound to catch sheefish. They also caught trout.

Each night the students had to prepare their catch for their meal. In the evening elders taught beading and skin sewing. It was a first time experience for some of the students, who were more used to television and roaming the village in the evenings.

After a couple of weeks it was over. 'It's been another great success, even though I'm exhausted,' Kotzman wrote to me. 'Elmer and I are definitely planning more camps.'

I was impressed by the way Kotz had hung around in his holidays to address the kids' needs. He sounded like a very special person. Someone I would have liked to work for.

I was heading back to Sydney during the July school holidays for

Ella's 21st. I was excited to be going back for my promised visit.

Meanwhile, Kotzman was preparing to head off to visit his son and daughter. We would not have communication for a few weeks.

Ella's 21st was a wonderful celebration held at a restaurant in Potts Point, Sydney. She looked so beautiful. So grown up. I felt reassured that our move had been positive for her. Ella had settled into the city routine with work and socialisation. She seemed to have become quite worldly. She looked happy.

I used my free time during the days to catch up with friends. I missed Paratai. She was from the Tainui tribe and was in the North Island of New Zealand visiting family. Leena was busy at work, and we only had time for a brief catch-up. I didn't mention Kotzman or the website match dot com to her, but we talked about everything else.

I stayed at a backpackers around the corner from Ella's apartment. I felt like a stranger in the middle of this big city. I was disconnected from this café culture after six months of living in the country. Even though I had my Australian citizenship, I definitely felt like a tourist. Gauche. I really liked that.

I was ready to return to my quiet country life. And with news of Kotz's holiday to go back to, I had something to look forward to on my return.

Kotzman was on holiday throughout June and July. Over that time he had visited family and brought his nephew back to visit Elmer's fish camp. He had also had some special time with his grandchildren, whom he sorely missed.

After Kotz and I returned from our travels, we started using a chatting format. We could chat through a chat room that enabled our conversations to flow back and forth.

Alaskaman had first introduced me to the method during the time Kotzman was away. I had then shared it with Kotz on his return. It made the emailing much more immediate. Much more like a conversation.

We had emailed our impressions of our holidays. Kotz wrote that his daughter had thought it 'cute' he had met someone from New Zealand. However she wanted him to keep on looking for another contact for a proper relationship. Someone closer.

'Well,' wrote Kotzman, 'with the amount of emailing I am doing, as well as getting school started again, there isn't time for any other relationship.'

I laughed. Yes, emailing did take time, and I was also up to my ears in work and study again.

The new school year was beginning mid August in Kotzebue. Kotzman was worried about whether the entire faculty would actually turn up. Often new hires did not show.

'You know, unbelievable as it may sound,' he wrote, 'faced with the reality of working out in isolated bush Alaska, teachers do back out at the last moment.'

'Wow, that's amazing.'

'Even after signing written contracts.'

'Any penalty?'

'Well, if they are already in Alaska they risk having their certification pulled. If they're from the Lower 48, then they will have jeopardised any future application for Alaska certification.'

'Oh, right.'

'Finding a replacement at short notice early in the school year through the Alaska Teacher Placement agency can be very difficult.' I kept thinking about people not actually showing up after signing their contract. In Balclutha, that didn't bear thinking about. But out there was even more remote. What would they do?

'Sometimes untrained locals have to fill in till someone else is found,' Kotzman wrote. 'Schedules then have to be rearranged last moment to ensure that a certified teacher is present in all classes. That is the law.'

Kotz had hired a new counsellor and had decided to relinquish his principal's comfortable apartment in order to make the package more attractive for the counsellor to move to Kotzebue.

Elmer had offered him a small cabin in the middle of the native village area of Kotzebue. It was a place where Elmer did some carving in a small workshop. Kotzman and Mato both moved there.

'Really the cabin is survivable, not extensively comfortable. The fixing up will happen in due time.' He reassured me that he much preferred living there than in the *gussaq* area of town. 'It feels more real, and I feel safer.' He explained, 'I am looked after here. Elmer says there's a pride in the locals about having their principal living amongst them.'

I could imagine that.

'You know other areas of Kotzebue have recently been vandalised. The "Kotzebue National Forest", a nurtured one-tree stand, was annihilated in one fell swoop!' Both Native Alaskans and *gussaqs* had been equally outraged. It sounded like village living could be unpredictable. Even dangerous.

Chapter 19

Back to Pilot Station

Mid-afternoon, Margaret drove me out to Mountain Village airport in the district truck, stopping first at the post office. I was learning that the post office, with its rows of household post boxes, was a hugely important place in the bush.

Margaret came back out waving a package. 'Parcel from home!' She looked happy as she plonked herself down behind the driver's seat. There was a bundle of letters gathered with a rubber band and a handwritten post box number scrawled over the front. She looked again at the writing on the front of the parcel. 'From my sister. I wonder what she has sent me this time!' I could hear the anticipation in her voice as her eyes wandered from the parcel and back to the road ahead.

In the bright daylight of the afternoon sun I could now see all the buildings in Mountain Village were up on stilts. I asked Margaret about it.

'It's because of the permafrost,' she explained. 'Some villages further north from us have permanently frozen ground.' I knew the Arctic Circle did. 'Here the ground freezes and then thaws again in the warmer temperatures. It makes the ground unstable. All the constant moving causes foundations to buckle and collapse.' She chatted on, 'Building houses up on piles like this allows cool air to circulate beneath. Makes them stronger.'

The piles were made of special material and filled with non-freezing liquid. During the changing seasons they absorbed heat or cold from the ground and maintained more stability.

In Pilot Station the newer houses had been built on piles. Many thought the Eskimo people still lived in igloos. I remembered I had thought that when writing to Kotzman. I now knew that igloos were not used as dwelling places any more. They were sometimes built by hunters on long expeditions as survival shelters.

A Yup'ik woman told me she had been taught as a child, 'Quiet voices not melt ice on igloo ceiling.' Culturally this was another reason for few words.

Margaret received a message over the VHF in the truck. 'Plane landing in five'. We were almost at the airstrip. I would be on time.

As the plane landed at Mountain Village I noticed how suddenly a swarm of four-wheelers appeared and buzzed over to it. It didn't seem to matter if you had a booking or not. Whenever a plane landed there were people wanting to travel. Many had family in neighbouring villages, and in this still variable weather before the first snow, planes were the only way to get there. I had been told, 'First on, first seated.'

Margaret bounced the truck over to the plane. The pilot was offloading cargo. Some of the four-wheelers were already scurrying off with boxes he had passed them. Other passengers stood by the steps waiting for the word to get on. There was not much time between landing and leaving. I was still learning. Margaret got out of the truck and walked over to the pilot. I could see her talking to him and he nodded. She passed him my bag. I was not missing this flight.

'Come on.' With a quick kiss on her icy cheek, I was boarding. The plane was already full. We were off.

On this direct flight back to Pilot Station I noticed some major changes in the landscape already. September's fall had been beautifully coloured. Now, almost two weeks later in early October, the colours were noticeably muted. Those bright autumnal colours of my first flight were now dull. Deep olive-green conifers accented the yellowing grey-brown of dying tundra. Grey and tan muddy slopes dropped into deepening grey rivers.

Seasons were fast changing here. The freeze up and the snow would not be far away.

I landed safely back at Pilot Station. Gary was there to greet me, all smiles and warm hugs again. We drove back down to the house in the rapidly cooling evening. Gary told me he had been given a parcel of moose meat from one of the high school students.

'It's the middle of moose-hunting season, honey.' He grinned. 'All the village men are gone.' He was animated. 'There's real excitement in the air!'

Each household hoped to have a moose, as the meat would last all winter. Everyone was looked after in the village. Younger family members caught moose for their elders. Fathers and sons helped uncles catch theirs.

'Someone has just caught a 50-inch spread,' Gary chatted.

'What does that mean?'

'Fifty inches, that's more than a 120 centimetres, between the horns. That's a good bull-moose specimen. Plenty of eating off that.' I could see the hunter-gatherer exposed in Gary. He was definitely into all of this.

'You know, honey,' he continued. 'The boy that got the moose wanted to go back out and "catch" another one.'

'Catch the moose?' I asked. 'Did they really catch one, and then kill it?'

'No, no. The native Alaskans believe the spirit of an animal can hear you. If you brag about killing an animal, they believe it might hear that bragging and not sacrifice itself to you.' He looked at me to see if I understood. 'So they say catch not kill.'

Hunting was done with great respect for the animal. I liked that.

As I settled back at our home over the delicious pot roast of beef Gary had prepared, he talked of a boating trip he had planned for us the coming weekend. We would go only if the weather was safe for travelling. A couple of the local villagers wanted to take their boat to visit family. They needed to do that before the river froze over. A group of teachers had banded together offering to pay for the fuel if they could come along and pick up some groceries.

I was interested in seeing what the stores in St Mary's might offer. I wanted to make some Anzac biscuits, or cookies as they were known in America. I had visited the small store at Pilot Station down near the river one day – the store I had seen on my unforgettable trip to the elementary school. The big wooden room was sparse in its supplies. The low shelves held only limited amounts of anything. Everything was coated with a fine dust. Expiration dates had no meaning. Dates had ranged back over five and more years. I noticed bolts of material, for *quspuks* I guessed, and many cans of 'pop' or fizzy drink stacked in boxes along the floor. It was disturbing to see this type of junk food for sale. Especially here in a place where the only quality food source for generations had been subsistence hunting and gathering.

At the Pilot Station store I had bought sugar, desiccated coconut, two packets of Jell-O for a sore throat that had been developing, a box of tissues for the same reason, one ice-cream, a popsicle on a stick, butter, four glasses, some golden syrup or corn syrup, a tin of fruit and some deeply-frozen strawberries. That had been almost $US80. Expensive.

So an excursion by boat to St Mary's and some grocery shopping were definitely appealing. It might be the last chance to travel and stock the cupboards before 'freeze up'.

I thought back to that earlier New Zealand summer.

Chapter 20

Summertime in New Zealand

Kotzman was online. 'Sunshine, I am thinking of heading to Mexico for some sun over the Christmas winter break.'

Everywhere in New Zealand there was news of the upcoming millennium, and how we in New Zealand would be seeing the sun first. Without hesitation I wrote back.

'You should come here. We will be welcoming in the millennium first in New Zealand.'

Kotz's response was immediate. 'That sounds like a great plan! Would that be okay?'

Oh my goodness, what have I just said? 'Sure,' I responded, and logged off.

Sitting quietly in my chair I thought about what had just transpired. I had not shared this internet contact with anyone, and now Kotzman might actually show up! What would I say? How would I explain him? Goodness, I wouldn't even know him if I fell over him. He hadn't seen any pictures of me either. This was getting a bit too up close and personal. Complicated. I logged back on.

'Sorry, technical glitch.'

'Sunshine, I would really like to come, but you need some time to think about it. I don't want to cause any problems.' He knew I was living in a small rural community. I was a new import myself. But I had come from Sydney, from wide life experience. I thrived on a challenge. I thought, no small community mindedness is going to put *me* off.

'It will be fine,' I wrote without much conviction. 'Check out the flights and see if it is actually feasible to come all the way out of Kotzebue. With your frequent blizzards and unreliable flight times it might be impossible.' Getting to New Zealand and back in time for school restarting would be very difficult. I felt more hopeful. He probably couldn't do it.

'Great! Will do,' he wrote, and signed off.

Over the next couple of days the reality of Kotzman possibly coming all the way from the Arctic sank in. He was a man who knew more about me than anyone. Someone I had shared my innermost private thoughts with. I had been so certain we would never meet. I had felt so utterly safe. My Alaska mountain man. How could Kotzman possibly walk into my own little Balclutha reality?

He wrote several days later, 'I've found a flight that'd do it out of here, Sunshine. There's a bit of a layover in LA but I'd get to you by 18 Dec.' He wasn't wasting time looking. 'Looks good for getting back too.'

Kotzman wrote several times to check me out. Was I still okay about him coming? He seemed to be getting very excited.

'Hey Sunshine, I found out I can be there for the new millennium *and* leave in time to get back for the second semester early January. Great, huh?'

In Kotzebue it was now dark nearly 24 hours a day. The snow came in with such force the housing was sometimes covered by blown snow in the morning. Perhaps he would be snowed in, I thought hopefully. The more enthusiastic he became, the more despondent I was feeling.

'I might even get some time to see part of the South Island in the summer! Get a tan!' he wrote. He would also, of course, have a chance to meet me.

Meantime he sent me a photo by email. He had the school librarian take it especially. We'd never thought about meeting, so physical appearance hadn't been a consideration before now. As his photo rolled off my printer and into my room, it was as if a total stranger had entered my life. The man who gradually appeared grinning from out of my printer was definitely *not* the man I had imagined. He was older, balding and sitting in a computer chair in a checked sports coat. I was devastated. This was Kotzman? My wild Alaska Man? The man with long windswept hair that lived in a cave and walked around in skins clutching a knife between his teeth! This *couldn't* be him. I gulped. Too late now.

'Sunshine, can you send me a photo of you please? I bet you are as lovely as you sound!' Blimey. Pressure. I pulled out every photo I could find, searching for the worst one I had. If he was not put off by that photo, I thought, maybe he would be pleasantly surprised when he actually met me.

'The photo is in the snail mail today,' I wrote a few days later. 'I've sent it to you care of the school.' More public disclosure, I thought. This was not the private little *tete-à-tete* I loved anymore. It was bridging into consciousness. Everyone's consciousness.

I started preparing people for the news. Their responses were fast and pointed.

'You have been doing *what*?'

'You are meeting someone from the *internet*! Emma! I thought you had more sense!'

My father was the worst. 'He's coming from *Alaska* you say? Well, he must be desperate,' he had muttered before returning to dig hard in his vegetable patch.

Kotzman went ahead with the flights. I booked a motel for him on the opposite side of Christchurch from my parents' house. I would drive up from Balclutha to meet him, take him to his motel and I would stay across town with my parents. I was filled with resignation about this whole thing.

'What are you going to be wearing when you arrive?' I emailed him several days later without much enthusiasm. I needed to know so I could pick him out in the crowd. His response made my stomach fall.

'I thought I'd wear my Levis, baseball cap and cowboy belt and buckle. Easy to pick,' he wrote enthusiastically. Cowboy belt and buckle, and baseball cap! I decided then and there I could go no further. This was fast going from bad to worse. I had to call this whole developing mess off.

I tossed and turned at night, talking seriously with myself. What are you thinking? Relax! You're not getting into a relationship. I was realising that I had invested more emotion into all of this than I had thought. You're just showing a good friend around. He is a great guy, you know him very well. In fact you know him better than most of your friends here. For goodness sake, what does it matter what he is *wearing*?

I was surprised by my shallowness, as if looks were all that mattered. I thought you were better than that! I scolded myself. However, I was learning that it was more than looks. It was more about showing my cards to the world. Maybe it was a hand filled with duds. Reluctantly, each morning I continued with my plans.

I had written in one of my earlier emails that my father owned an MGBGT. Apparently Kotz used to own a sports car in another life a long time ago.

'An MG?' Kotzman had responded. 'Wow. That is my dream car! I've always wanted to ride in one of those.' Now he emailed to say that he had only one request of me. Could he have a ride in my father's MG?

'Sure,' I responded unenthusiastically. I wondered if he was checking if my father actually *did* own an MG, if I had been telling the truth.

Meanwhile Kotzman had received my photo. I thought he was overly enthusiastic about how I looked. I was quietly starting to think along the same lines as my father.

Kotz had sounded excited in his last email. 'At least I already have a passport thanks to that advice from Charles,' he wrote. 'Imagine trying to get a passport organised from here!' An old friend had suggested getting a passport a couple of years previously. 'Hey buddy, makes sense. Never know when you might need it,' his friend Charles had said. Kotzman had never travelled internationally before.

'I'll be fine, Sunshine, as long as there are no blizzards in Kotzebue to stop the flight out.' Blizzards were now a daily occurrence. He chatted on. 'I have my CD player and a couple of good books. I'll stick close to the information booths for my flight times.'

Blizzards were my last hope. 'I can't wait!' he wrote.

I could.

Chapter 21

Up the Yukon

Saturday morning in Pilot Station dawned foggy and still. It looked as if it would be fine enough for travel. I woke up coughing. James, Gary's deputy assistant, had dropped off a snowsuit for me to try on for size. Although my coughing hadn't got any worse, no one wanted to take any chances on this boat trip.

I had noticed how everyone genuinely looked out for everyone else's health. The interdependence between the staff developed quickly when living far from medical supplies and the usual medical support. There was a medical centre in the village, but *gussaqs* had been warned by their doctors in Anchorage to stay away from village medical centres.

Local villagers were trained in first aid to become the medical centre's 'medical workers'. However there were stories of people becoming severely ill through being given the wrong medication. I had heard that the equipment in the medical centre at Pilot Station was a one-ring electric burner. If a serious medical alarm was raised, there could always be a bush plane flight out to the native hospital in Bethel. Or a Black Hawk helicopter in.

We had no water. The water problem had been occurring ever since my arrival. Everyone told me it was a perennial problem. Most teachers had large stocks of water stored in their cupboards. Because of the expense of flying water in, seasoned faculty put buckets outside to catch whatever rainwater they could. Rainwater while it still rained, that is. They suggested we do the same before freeze-up.

Village water was renowned for contamination. I had seen the broken pipelines down by the elementary school. When tested by the officials who flew in periodically, faecal matter was often found in the drinking water. The water didn't seem to bother the locals, just those new to this lifestyle. Gary had a small distiller that he recommended we use for drinking water.

Washing didn't matter so much. I would need to go down to the school for a shower when we got back. The school had an independent water supply.

Our neighbours Tim and Anna were coming with us. As principal, Gary had the luxury of using the school's four-wheel-drive truck in the weekends, although there wasn't far to travel in it. One trail up and down from the airport to the river with a side trail to the new school near the top. That was the extent of it. Winter snow offered much greater travelling opportunities. The four of us loaded up in the truck, and Gary drove the bumpy trail back down past the elementary school to the river.

Skiffs and small outboard motor boats were pulled in along the riverbank. The boats were used to go fishing or visiting. Petrol was so expensive out here. Barged in over the summer, it was subsequently delivered to small storage tanks at the store or at communal meeting places. The people here did not go joy-riding in their boats. Most of the boats stayed up on the bank most of the time.

James was already at the boat helping Joe and his son fuel up. We were travelling on a skiff about 20 feet long. At the back there was a small, raised, wooden standing box with white peeling paint. Joe would be steering the boat from in there. James, Joe and his son were carrying large petrol cans and stacking them in the boat. With us all on board it would be heavy. I hoped we wouldn't sink.

It was critical that we took fuel supplies.

'Never want to run out of fuel out there,' James waved his hand around, indicating the local scenery. There were plenty of spare parts aboard, Gary had told me. We needed to be prepared in case we broke down.

Joe had a small handheld VHF radio. The village would know we were leaving for St Mary's. There would be a silent watch held out till we arrived back at our estimated return time of 3 pm.

The teachers had all brought large tubs to carry the supplies back in. We would be getting some groceries for the other faculty too. I was getting used to seeing these large 20-litre plastic bins. Bins and duct tape were popular out here in the bush. James had also brought along some chilly bins, or chest freezers as they were called there. The entire crowd had fallen about laughing at my New Zealand term 'chilly bin'.

'Hey, did you hear what Emma called this?' James shouted to Joe. 'A *chilly* bin!' He roared with laughter. Joe reacted in the typically native way. He gave a very small smile and a gentle nod with lowered eyes. He wouldn't deliberately make me feel uncomfortable. It made me wonder what the natives thought of these loud American *gussaqs*. What talk was had in their private homes at night about these foreigners who had charge over their children. If any talk at all. Words were scarce. To these people, actions were more important.

Although I had a scarf, Gary had given me a facemask to wear. 'Honey, you'll need it.' It had holes for my nose and a small opening for the mouth. It was held on with Velcro at the back of my head. I pulled my hat down over it. I was glad I hadn't been wearing *that* gear at LA airport. I looked like a bank robber and I felt self-conscious. No one appeared even slightly interested or even commented.

We were all so heavily rugged up that moving was difficult. It was like being dressed for the ski slopes. Then James passed out life jackets. We struggled to put them on over all the existing layers. None of the natives wore them but the *gussaqs* all did.

Some village men were on the bank to push us off. No waving, just quiet watching. Listening too. Eskimo were excellent at hearing micro shifts in changing sounds. Sometimes it was the listening that caught the moose, or the bad motor.

As we picked up speed along the river the wind chill hit me; it was like razor blades biting into the skin. Gary and Tim sat with their backs to the wind. They were blocking the worst of it from Anna and me, who sat facing forward. I was hoping to see where we were going, but my eyes were weeping in the cold behind my sunglasses. Anna and I huddled together. I could quickly see this was going to be another test of endurance.

Gary was pointing something out. His words were whipped from his mouth and flung into the wind. No point in talking. We reverted to gesturing, just like the natives. He and Tim saw some moose, and the men were all pointing and nodding together. I spent most of the trip staring at the bottom of the boat, huddled as low as I could.

Luckily I had thought to bring a thermos and some tea and coffee. Anna and I together managed to pour out the drinks for everyone. As the boat slapped up and down on the water it was hard to keep the contents in the cup.

We eventually passed the tiny settlement of Pitkas Point, which sat on the promontory to St Mary's. We turned and started to slow as we moved up the tributary to where St Mary's village was nestled. The relief at reaching our destination was great. We had covered eleven miles in 40 minutes.

The instant the boat started to slow the chill became manageable. We pulled up on a riverbank near some wooden steps that rose up a steep bank to the top. Joe's son leapt ashore and pulled the boat to a rail where he lashed it tight. Standing up was hard. I seemed to have frozen into a crouched statue. But many hands were offered to help me step over the boat's bow and onto the bank. I was back in St Mary's for the third time in two weeks.

There were two main stores in St Mary's. That had surprised me. From the air, all I had seen were the huts on the hill. The main part of the village, however, was set back along the river, away from the airstrip.

James had arranged with Joe what time we would meet back at the boat. We didn't want to be too long. Better to travel in the middle of the day. It would be warmer and it was easier to cope with emergencies in the daylight, should they happen. We left the empty tubs in the boat; we could put the groceries in them on our return.

'Hey, let's head for AC traders first,' said James. 'They sell hot food.' Corn dogs, corn battered sausages, were lined up in a small counter heater. Margaret had rung ahead and ordered some fried chicken pieces for James to bring back. It impressed me that she had known what to do.

'The hot food smells delicious, doesn't it,' Anna said, grinning at me.

'Yeah, I'm getting some, are you?' She nodded eagerly.

'Hey, hot coffee anyone?' asked Gary. We all bought hot food and hot coffee, and stood eating and drinking as the blood started to flow through our bodies again. I was beginning to think the trip was worth it just for this.

'Okay, shopping next,' I said to Anna and she nodded. We only had a limited amount of time and lots to do. Lumbering around the store in our heavy gear with small plastic shopping baskets didn't warrant any attention. There were only a couple of others there. I bought more supplies for the Anzac biscuits that were proving a big hit back in the village.

'Hey honey, let's stock up on the cranberry juice,' Gary said, eyeing the rows of red juice bottles. 'They'll be too heavy to fly in, and it'll make a great change from distilled water.' I agreed. We bought six large bottles of juice. We would collect them later on our way back down to the boat.

Anna and I lingered over the small cabinet at the counter that sold locally made jewellery. 'Just look at that beadwork,' I said pointing my gloved finger at the cabinet. The beadwork earrings were beautiful. 'I'm going to buy that small green pair. The ones that cost $15.' I paid the money and put them carefully in my pocket.

'You know, Emma, some of the women make them in our village. You can order them from them. Bracelets too,' Anna remarked. I decided to do that in the future. I'd seen all the women wearing beaded bracelets. I would love one. I also wanted to support the local economy where I could.

We wandered off to the Commercial Traders Company. The men wanted to check out the snow machines that were there. Gary had been talking about getting a snow machine, or sno-go as they were commonly known.

'Anna and I are going to get a sno-go each,' Tim announced. He and Anna had been discussing it at length. Flyers were in our post boxes.

'Margaret and I have a two-up,' James replied. 'Margaret prefers to stick with me when we go out on the snow trails.' I nodded. It seemed to me that the older faculty members went for the slow and steady transport. The young ones wanted independence and more fun. I looked at Gary.

'A two-up sounds fine by me.' He smiled, nodding in agreement.

'I think that's a good idea, honey.'

Nothing could be purchased till first snow had fallen anyway. The only way to bring a snow machine back from St Mary's to Pilot Station would be to ride it.

After wandering around a bit more, we lumbered back down to the boat. There was nothing much else to see in St Mary's. Joe and his son were waiting. They had had a good family visit. We stacked our groceries in the tubs and hunkered down for the ride back.

The boat trip back didn't seem as cold as the one there. I wondered if the expectation of freezing, subconsciously prepares the body to generate more warmth. Nevertheless, it was really good to round the bend and see Pilot Station again. The afternoon sun was liquid and the cold was penetrating.

We had bought provisions, had warmed up and had had a good look around. All in all it was therapy for us all. We offloaded. People appeared from nowhere and lent a hand. I loved the way people looked after each other like that.

After dropping off Tim and Anna and stacking up our purchases, we headed back to the school to shower.

'Water's still off,' Gary announced. He had checked the taps as soon as we got home. 'Word has it that it will be like that for a few more days.'

'Oh well,' I replied. I was getting to really understand the luxury of turning on a tap and having water pour forth. 'You know, I can't believe how much water we use each day,' I said. 'I never used to think about it before.' I conserved any water that we had, reusing it when possible. I had become very conscious of the quantities of water we needed for everything.

'Just part of the fun of daily living in the bush, babe,' Gary said, giving me a hug.

Chapter 22

A Visitor to Christchurch

Finally it was mid December and school was out for the long summer holidays. I was leaving Bel with my retired neighbours Merv and Evelyn. They loved minding Bel. She would walk over most days, sit on the front door step and wait for treats.

I headed on the six-hour journey up to Christchurch in my little white Mazda. I wanted to meet up with my long time girlfriend Jenny in Christchurch first. We had been in high school together and had made renewed contact since my return from Sydney. Jenny was sensible. She was my foil. She would be very helpful in the drama that was unfolding and shaking my world.

'When you get here, Em, come around and have some dinner. You can tell me all about this man. Sounds *very* exciting!' She'd sounded enthusiastic on the phone. I knew she was also pretty surprised at the whole thing. But Jenny and I went back a long way. I had been a bit of a wild card at school. The fact that I was obviously still a bit that way put us back on familiar ground. Tore away the years. Bound us in collusion again.

Settled over a glass of wine and fantastic meal – she was an excellent cook – I launched into the saga of Kotzman.

'Start from the beginning,' she said. 'Match dot com? What is that?' She was intrigued. 'You've been writing to him daily for months? What do you know about him?' Jenny never judged. She listened intently while I unravelled the saga. The wine went straight to my head, and I was in my element. Jenny was a responsive listener. I embellished the story and added juicy details to draw her into it.

'He was a solo dad,' I bragged, warming to the chance to build Kotz's character. To help her understand the man we were about to meet. 'Raised his two kids from babyhood.'

'Goodness,' Jenny was impressed. That sounded like a new age man. 'What happened to his wife?' I launched into an explanation of the unravelling of Kotz's marriage. They had been poles apart in parenting. He had been given custody. Kotz had been teaching fulltime during the later childrearing years.

'Yeah, he'll be pretty domesticated, I think.' I was actually enjoying this. Our evening of attempted serious discussion kept dissolving into wild schoolgirl giggling at the danger of it all. In the end I wasn't much further on.

'Bring him over as soon as possible for lunch!' She urged me. 'I'll tell you then what I think about all this!' More excited giggling. We had great fun that night.

December 18, 1999 dawned, and I dressed slowly in my light lemon jumper, long pants and sandals. The lemon jumper had been bought especially for this first meeting. I wanted at least a part of me to look like Kotzman's Sunshine. My long hair was carefully arranged to look casual. I had spent more time on the little daytime makeup I usually wore.

My parents were very aware of the enormity of this meeting for me. My mother was quite excited. 'You look lovely, dear,' my mother had surveyed me with sympathetic eye. 'Lovely jumper. That colour suits you.'

My father got the MG out and had it purring quietly outside the house. He had cleaned it again, and it was ready for the drive to the airport. I felt like I was on a roller coaster that had reached its summit and was now starting to run downhill.

I stepped into the car and he gave me specific instructions about handling his pride and joy. This was a pure bred. It needed specialised handling. My father was definitely a car man.

'Keep the choke right out for now, then push it in to the silver mark when you get into third. Okay?' He was leaning through the open driver's window. I nodded vaguely.

'When you change gear, remember to rev the car slightly for a smoother transition. And don't forget to drive into the corners. She runs smoother like that.' He stood back with his hands on his hips and grinned. None of this information was registering in my heightened anxious state of mind. 'Off you go!' He patted the car on the roof encouragingly, and we jumped forward.

I gave my father a distracted wave as we lurched off. I then proceeded to buck and jump my way to the airport. I admonished myself for taking this car on this first meeting. I had wanted to prove my honesty at the onset. The last thing I needed though was more stress.

The MG eventually found a bay in the car park near the terminal and immediately stalled. Sulked was more like it. I prayed in all my lip biting driving to the airport that I had not left lipstick on my front teeth.

Grabbing my bag, I locked the car with an authority I didn't feel. I needed to be boss of the situation. I had discouraged anyone from accompanying me to this meeting. I had had plenty of offers. There was much intrigue and discussion about this. Putting on my sunglasses, I marched into the domestic terminal as confidently as I could on shaky legs.

I was about to come face to face with a stranger. A man I knew very well, I just had never met him before. I wanted our initial meeting to be between only us. Just like our emails.

A quick composed scan of the flight board showed the plane was on time. I headed for a discreet seat. There was one vacant right behind a pillar. Perfect. Maybe I wouldn't stand up. Maybe I wouldn't reveal myself at all. I felt more in control. Sitting alone and behind the pillar, I tried to arrange my face in a peaceful manner.

My left eye was twitching wildly. It had been doing this for the last two weeks. It was a sure sign I was under pressure. I hoped it didn't look like I was winking at people, especially at men. I was in trouble enough. I stared into the middle distance. With about ten minutes to wait, I practised deep breathing.

I went over the mantra in my mind. I knew what to look for. I tried to relax. The clock seemed to be moving twice as fast as usual. Galloping along in two-minute intervals. Vague intercom announcements were only just audible. I wondered with rising panic if that last announcement was for the Auckland inbound plane. I waited, leaning forward slightly in anticipation.

As the glass doors glided back, a group of luggage toting passengers were discharged into the domestic airport. Loud laughter and talking back and forth confirmed Americans. I noticed that I was holding my breath. As I searched the crowd for any signs of Kotzman, I was dismayed to see that it seemed every second man was wearing a baseball cap, Levis and sporting a moustache.

Then, as my anxiety grew to the point of hyperventilation, a lone man walked through the doors and stopped. He reached into his jacket pocket and pulled out a large sheet of paper. I watched as he unfolded it and held it up for the world to see.

'I am from Alaska, and I need Sunshine!' it read. Oh my goodness, it's Kotzman! I leapt to my feet. He saw me immediately and grinned. Striding across the floor I snatched the piece of paper out of his hands. I was flushing hotly with terror and excitement. I was also grinning wildly, more from public embarrassment than anything else. So much for hiding.

'My, Sunshine, you're *tall*!' he laughed as he looked down at me. He said 'tall' to rhyme with 'doll'. He then spoke some foreign sounding words. 'That was Inuit and Shoshone for "Greetings",' he explained proudly. 'Bin practising all the way here!' He laughed again. He seemed nervous too.

Being tall was a sore point with me. It was all I could focus on. Tallest person at intermediate school was not far from the memory. He hates me, I thought.

'I need to sit down!' was all I could say.

'Sure,' he responded politely, finding a couple of vacant seats. As an aside he drawled, 'I've only been sittin' for 25 hours solid.'

After some small talk, we made our way over to the bag carousel, where he grabbed one bag. 'You know,' he chuckled, 'if you hadn't shown up, I had a plan B! I was gonna contact one of these travel agents and get a tour of Noo Zealand.' For all my cold feet and trepidation, I felt a bit indignant that he would have held any thoughts of my not showing up. Didn't he know I was an honourable person?

As Kotzman lugged his bag out across the car park he said quietly, 'My, you are gorgeous!' I guess the photo ploy worked. Or the jumper. Apparently I looked better than he expected. He did too. I blushed and was struck into silence. I couldn't think of one thing to say.

'Boy, that was a long haul from LA. Lucky I had my CD player and adventure books to keep me entertained.' Nodding and smiling idiotically, I responded to his quiet chatter. I was acutely aware he was trying to normalise the abnormal and I was grateful for his words. 'I made a nest in the plane and just stayed put.' He went on smoothly, 'Boy, I'm mighty glad to have got here!' He grinned at me.

Kotzman stopped dead at the sight of the deep maroon MGBGT. I must admit it did look pretty flash sitting there. It glinted in sleek smart lines. For the first time that day I was pleased with it.

'Um, I think we might have a bit of trouble squeezing everything in,' I said dubiously, looking at his large bag and backpack. I took out my keys and opened the hatch back.

'No problem!' he responded cheerfully, stuffing his bags in the back. We then did a little dance as he attempted to get in the driver's side with me. He had forgotten our cars were set up in reverse.

'Oh, excuse me!' he exclaimed chuckling. 'We're on the opposite side here, aren't we?' Laughing he opened my door for me. I tried to drop elegantly and casually into the bucket seat. Kotzman opened the passenger door and squeezed into the seat next to me. I was suddenly conscious now how close we were. Strapped like two eggs in a carton, shoulder to shoulder.

My father's instructions regarding the correct sequence for starting the car were gone from my brain. As it burst into life, the car recognised my touch and so we bucked and jumped all the way out to the toll-gate. Kotz was very sweet in trying to deflect this uncomfortable closeness and my inexperienced driving.

'My, look at all the sheep over there,' he remarked, staring intently out of his car window at the paddocks surrounding the airport. Beads of perspiration dripped quietly from under my arms.

I managed to find his motel and dropped him there.

'I'll come back in a couple of hours,' I explained. He had said he needed a rest. So did I. I was keen to get some time alone. 'I'll be back around two and take you to the gardens.'

When I got home, I was limp from the excitement and nervousness of it all. My mother was waiting at the door. 'Well dear, what's he like?'

'Good, I think,' was my reply. I was still trying to get my head around it all.

Chapter 23

First Snow at Pilot Station

Gary woke me in the morning. 'Snow, honey!' he shouted. We had had our first snowfall in Pilot Station and the landscape was completely changed. No rubbish or junk to be seen anywhere, just pristine white. It really did look just like a Christmas card.

Although it was early morning, locals were already out on their snow machines. I could hear them screaming past on the track. Most of the snow would be melted off by midday, and they knew to use what was on the ground now to go exploring. Snow meant freedom from the confines of village life.

Snow in Tutalgaq also meant treacherous conditions. When it rained the sleet would turn the surface to ice. I was virtually housebound through fear of falling. Gary had borrowed a pair of ice cleats for me. I could strap the cleats to my gumboots and manage to stay mostly upright. The first time I wore my gumboots in these new icy conditions was nearly my last. Even though I had on three pairs of socks my feet nearly froze solid inside the rubber. I underlined 'warm boots' on the list of the gear and provisions I would need on my return.

I had been hosting some dinner parties for faculty and staff. I had wanted to make sure I had seen everyone. There were only a few days left before I was due to leave.

Over the next few nights our house was abuzz with social banter. By the time I had finished my entertaining round, there weren't too many working at Pilot Station School that had not tasted Emma's Chicken Marengo.

It was an easy dish to prepare, and I found with the local dried cranberries added to a thick syrup sauce, chicken on rice with some frozen vegetables was easy, palatable and looked colourful. Locally bought ice cream, obviously refrozen several times but covered with frozen strawberries, was a popular dessert.

Anzac biscuits, now always referred to as cookies, were always served with tea and coffee afterwards. The men would lean forward from their chairs and with a glint of joy bordering on greed, pick up three or four at a time. I was baking batches of 40 nearly every other day.

It was during these party times that I learned much more about the local villagers and about the *gussaq* teachers that had come to work here.

'You know, Emma,' Heather, the kindergarten teacher, commented one evening after a shared meal, 'Eskimo dancing is starting again in the local cultural centre.'

'Oh really?' That very much interested me.

'Yes,' Heather replied. 'I have been before.' Heather offered to pick me up on her four-wheeler one evening and take me along. I was excited.

We had passed the low, domed, beehive-shaped building down in the village on our trips down to the river. I was looking forward to the opportunity to go inside. People from other villages often came to the centre during the winter months. Dancing for each other was an exciting and much anticipated treat for the native people.

We arrived about 7 pm. Some of the teenagers from the high school were standing around the entrance smoking. I nodded as I passed them. Inside, the drumming had already started. I could hear it as we approached.

On entering I could see benches that ran around the curved wall. The room was completely wooden. The shape was reminiscent of a very large igloo. I saw a small group of seven men sitting along a section of the seating. They were holding drums that they tapped with long sticks. There was one male amongst them chanting to the beat. Each drum was shaped rather like a tennis racket, a circle with a long handle. Skin was stretched across it.

Facing them, and dancing to the beat, were a group of women in *quspuks*. They stood in a slightly curved line. The women wore *mukluks*, long skin boots. On their heads were headdresses of fur and beads. The headdresses were tied around the head and low over the forehead. The beading hung in a fringe across the forehead and dropped down each side of the face. It reminded me of photos I had seen of Native American Indian chiefs.

Heather and I sat down just inside the entrance. The scene that unfolded under the subdued lighting was timeless. There was a strong smell of wood and wood smoke in the atmosphere. I could see that this was serious and important business. I felt so privileged to be able to sit and watch.

Children were part of the performing group. Girls stood in front holding small fans and imitated the women's movements. Young boys beating small drums sat cross-legged on the dusty wooden floor in front of the drumming men.

The drumming and chanting lifted and fell around several notes. It was mesmerising, so ancient in its sound. As the men chanted and drummed, the women were silent. They were bent at the knees bobbing up and down in time with the rhythm. In their hands they held small dance fans made of caribou tails. They brushed the air with the fans as they moved to the chanting. Each brush stroke appeared to tell another part of the story. It was all done in sequence and together.

As the dancing continued into the second hour, the dances seemed to shift in their mood and become more jovial. I wondered if these dances were practised as a release from the tension and concentration of the earlier ones.

The men appeared to tease the women by continually going back to what appeared to be the same chorus. They did this over and over again. It seemed as if any drumming man could initiate the repetition. Just when you thought the dance must finally come to a stop, yet another long round would begin. When that happened all the men would stare ahead and grin.

Gradually the tempo would speed up until the dancers were moving at great speed. The women's faces glowed with the exertion of this aerobic activity, but not one of their facial expressions would change. As if being wound up like a large clock, the dance would continue, with caribou tails sweeping in fast sequence. Each bob was choreographed to perfection, and with a particular expression.

The women gave no clue to how they felt about yet another round. They would simply increase the speed of their intricate movements, bobbing and waving with vigour. When the lead drummer finally rolled his drum to stop, everyone would collapse in fits of laughter.

Sometimes during the release and laughter, the drummer would pick up his drum and immediately start to beat a slow rhythm. Everyone would immediately make formation and begin again. It was like a military training exercise. Once again I was so in awe of these people and their skills. I was learning a very important part of the culture. Endurance, discipline, cooperation and humour.

Much later in the evening, Heather and I were asked to join in. Heather had danced before and had pre-warned me. Although I felt reluctant and nervous I knew it was rude not to at least try. I would give these people an opportunity for a good laugh at a clumsy *gussaq*.

Someone passed me some spare fans and I soon gave the group plenty of opportunity for laughter. Their laughter wasn't critical at all, more amusement in watching a small child trying to feed itself for the first time. The kind of laughter that happened when the child's spoon went to the eye rather than the mouth.

I really enjoyed myself, bobbing and waving along. Here I was standing in the middle of an ancient culture with local Yup'ik Eskimo people and dancing along. I was often completely out of time with everyone else. It was very much like learning a Maori action song. Learn by watching and copying. The more you watched and mimicked the moves, the better you got. No one stopped and deliberately showed you.

When we got up to dance, I noticed that some of the teenagers that had been standing around the doorway came in and sat down silently to watch. When we finished they merged back out into the night. These teenagers didn't say much. With dark hoodies and heads bowed they were more like monks. The only recognition was slightly raised eyebrows if they saw you.

There was bootlegging and drugs in the village, and Gary was often called on to deal with students' difficult behaviour. Even though as principal he was the ultimate in the disciplinary process, he somehow managed to maintain excellent rapport with the students. It was good for me to see first hand his operating style, a quiet talk and the start of a friendship. He also spent much time in low-key meetings with parents and grandparents, relationship building to try to figure a way through.

Chapter 24

Introducing Kotzman

It was strange wandering around Christchurch's Botanical Gardens with a man I had hardly seen but who spoke in familiar phrases and knew so much about me.

'So *this* is the Avon River you were telling me about,' Kotz observed as the green stream eddied around the bend, lit by dappled sunlight that shone through the willows. A punter paddled a couple along. She was trailing her hand in the water. 'Well, Sunshine, now I get what you meant about it having an old English feel.'

I kept shooting him little sideways glances, to check him out. This was he. Kotzman. If I didn't look at him and only listened, it was all very familiar. His turn of phrase. The topics. However, if I looked at him he still looked like a complete stranger. Weird.

'I've brought these cameras to take some snapshots of the place. Plants and greenery,' he explained. He had a couple of cameras, one film and one digital, strung around his neck. He seemed to be taking photos of everything. Well, all the things that were near me.

'Oh, what a pretty flower!' He enthused, bending to take a close up of a brilliant yellow rose.

'That's a rose like I was telling you about. It's just like the one I planted at my kitchen window in Balcutha.'

'Really . . . uh huh.' Another shot. He seemed to be taking heaps of photos. This rose, that tree, and so on. 'Oh wow, look at these plants all in a row. I *love* 'em.' He'd said plants like pants. They spoke like that in Australia too.

'They're hedges,' I explained. Kotzman didn't seem to know about hedges.

'Oh yeah. I saw those flying in this morning. They're all around the fields and gardens,' he exclaimed in wonder, taking more photos of the hedges.

'They're good windbreaks,' I responded. 'We get those nor' westers here I was telling you about. You need some protection from that wind.'

He nodded, snapping away again. Later I had found out that when Kotzman returned from his trip to New Zealand he had asked the librarian in Kotzebue to develop his prints. She had been intrigued to see that most of the principal's photos contained images of a woman. That had got them talking up in the Arctic Circle!

We spent several hours wandering around the gardens, taking in the art gallery and sharing a few laughs. By that time we were both feeling much more relaxed with each other. Poor Kotz, now his trial was really going to begin.

'As you know, we have dinner with Mum and Dad tonight,' I reminded him.

'Oh yeah, that's right,' he responded with a small smile. 'I've brought an atlas of Alaskan maps for your dad.' I could see Kotzman was a little nervous. I had already written to him of my father's seeming disapproval of this Alaskan mountain man. 'I think the gazetteer might interest him.' He looked to see my response.

'He'll love it,' I replied with a conviction I didn't feel.

We drove back from the gardens to my parents' house in my own little white Mazda, and arrived for dinner around 5 pm. After the introductions were made, Kotz gave my mother a box that contained small ivory earrings. He then passed the large atlas to my father.

'Thought you might enjoy this, sir,' he smiled.

'Good thinking!' said Dad. 'Now show me exactly where you live.'

I was amazed to see my father down on the floor with Kotzman poring over the book of maps. Only five minutes had elapsed since meeting. They were deep in conversation. So relieved was I at this immediate connection that I whispered to Mum, 'I'm just going for a quick walk over to the park.' I needed some fresh air and a break from all this conversation.

On my return 30 minutes later they were still chatting. My father had poured them all a wine. 'Come and have a look at this,' he said excitedly to me when I came back into the room, and Kotzman gave me a quick wink. Soon I was absorbed in the details of the Alaskan topography. We were in for a pleasant relaxed dinner and evening.

'You know, dear,' my father said to me later, after I had dropped Kotzman back to his motel and returned home. 'I've never met anyone more like you in my life.'

I decided to take that as a compliment.

As promised, I had arranged for us to visit Jenny for lunch. The following day I picked up Kotzman and we drove to her house. He was still enthusiastic about everything.

'You know, Sunshine, this place is absolutely stunning. I feel so at home already! And everyone is so doggone friendly. The people at the motels have been telling me about places to visit.'

When we arrived at her door Jenny met us, holding back her golden retriever, Honey. This beautiful and much loved pet was as enthusiastic as her owner about visitors to the door. Honey took some restraining.

'Well, hullo there,' Jenny greeted us with a big smile. 'Goodness, you have come a long way. This is Honey. Please excuse her jumping. She's quite excited.' She's not the only one, I thought.

Kotzman loved his own golden retriever Mato and he immediately felt a bond with Honey. It was hard to believe that this fantasy man was now actually standing in Jenny's house.

Jenny's Kiwi accent and Kotz's slight deafness, exacerbated by the long flight, combined to make conversation between them quite difficult. With a glass of bubbly firmly in my hand, I watched the scene unfolding like a Laurel and Hardy sketch.

'So what can I get you?' Jenny asked him.

'Excuse me,' he looked a bit stunned. 'Get you?'

'To drink.'

'Drenk?'

I was absolutely no help at all. I was standing back snorting to myself. They politely struggled on with the niceties, while Honey bounding between them became a useful distraction.

'Excuse me,' Kotz said eventually. 'My hearin's a bit shot after the long flight. Mind if I sit in here?' Kotzman moved into the adjoining lounge.

'Of course,' Jenny sounded relieved.

Jenny and I retreated to the open kitchen for the final preparations of lunch. I hid myself away on a stool within Jenny's pantry with my glass of bubbly in hand. From there I could giggle unabatedly and pull faces at her from within.

'Stop it!' she glared, shooting me warning glances. She was trying hard to maintain polite conversation with Kotzman from the kitchen. She then succumbed herself, giggling quietly as she cut and chopped the salad with her back to him.

'How's the motel?' she ventured.

'Excuse me?' he responded, trying to calm Honey with one arm and concentrate at the same time.

'Where you're staying,' she explained.

'Oh, just in here, if that's okay.'

In the end the conversation deteriorated into Jenny or Kotzman repeating 'Excuse me?' to each other.

Jenny tried again, 'So tell me again, what was the weather like?' I guffawed into the cinnamon and pepper pots. This whole thing was surreal.

Suddenly Kotzman spoke, stunning us both by speaking quite slowly and clearly. 'Excuse me, but would you mind if I bit Honey on the muzzle?'

Jenny and I gaped at each other. What? I immediately appeared from within the confines of the pantry, the better to hear this conversation.

'Can I bite y' dog on the muzzle, just gently? Might help her settle.' Maybe I needed a bite too, I thought.

'Yes, of course,' Jenny replied, more out of politeness than conviction. Was this a good idea? I needed to see this!

As we watched together, Kotzman got down on the floor. He placed his mouth crosswise over the dog's muzzle. Then he gently closed his mouth. Honey immediately sat. Kotz then got up and looked at us both staring at him wide-eyed. With a small grin he asked, 'Okay if I take her outside in the garden?'

'Yes, of course.' Jenny's record was stuck. She nodded with much more conviction than she felt. I too nodded distractedly, amazed.

'Honey.' Kotz called the dog. He moved away first, while Honey waited politely then followed at heel after him. They stepped outside together.

'Blimey,' I muttered. Through the window we could see Kotzman giving basic hand commands. Honey was settled and compliant.

'Come back anytime!' Jenny called gaily as we drove off after lunch.

'Kotz, what on earth were you doing with that thing with Honey?' I asked on our drive back to his motel.

'Oh, the muzzle thing?' He checked my face. 'It's a technique used to assert alpha male dominance,' he explained. 'Dogs are part of the wolf pack. They get it.'

Alpha male dominance indeed. From that moment onwards, in Jenny's eyes Kotzman could do no wrong.

That visit had been another completely overwhelming success.

Chapter 25

Preparing to Leave

Gary had a principal's conference in Anchorage mid October. He and I would fly out together. I would fly on home to New Zealand from Anchorage the following day. I was excited that I would have a companion on my next bush flight. It would help me relax and just enjoy the scenery. With Gary in charge I wouldn't need to worry about unexpected landings and weather hold-ups. It felt deeply comforting to be travelling some of the route together. It also eased the prospect of impending separation.

The first snow had melted again. The sporadic late morning four-wheelers that drove past our lounge room window no longer intrigued me. It was now a familiar scene. Old folk, mothers and babies constantly made their way up and down the same muddy track for mail, plane flights and visiting. The men always seemed to be away on important business. Hunting.

I had called home several times to speak to Ella and my parents. They were now aware of our plans. I still remembered my first call where I was madly excited about Alaska. My parents had asked, 'You *are* coming back, aren't you?' I had had to break my news very gently.

We had already made bookings for my return mid January. Gary wanted me to fly with him at Christmas over to Champaign in the Mid West and meet his family. We would then fly back to Alaska together. I would be missing the summer in New Zealand. I kept the thoughts of resigning, packing and leaving New Zealand mostly buried for now. I would save that for my flight home and face it on my return.

I chose the warmest part of the day immediately after lunch to pick my way carefully down to the post office and check for mail. I had strapped my ice cleats to my gumboots and added an extra pair of thermal socks. I was determined not to fall if I hit a frozen patch again. I was past being self-conscious; staying upright was far more important. Anyway this wasn't a culture of ridicule.

'*Waqaa*, Emma,' the postmaster said as I clacked my way loudly across the patchy Lino floor. Villagers quietly looked through their lowered eyebrows to see who was making all this noise.

'*Waqaa*, Wassillie.' I nodded to him, opened my post box to see if there was any mail of interest. Wassillie was one of the drummers. 'Any boxes for collection?'

The postmaster was the most popular man in the village. Everything of importance was flown in and passed out from the post office. As well as the regular mail, there were always 20-litre plastic tubs of food, clothing, mechanical parts, and cartons of all shapes and sizes containing all sorts of purchases. The postmaster needed strong arms. There was always much lifting to be done.

The Alaska Permanent Dividend Fund was due out in October, and everyone was planning on spending the cash payout. This fund was set up in 1976 to pay Alaskan residents a share of oil revenues. The total was usually around \$US1000 per person a year. Large families generated enough money annually to buy the latest snow machine or TV satellite dish. Some flew to visit relatives. Not many saved their money.

The flyers in our post boxes were all targeted for Alaska Permanent Dividend Fund big ticket spending. Snow machines, enormous television sets, hunting gear and winter clothing from Cabelas, the outdoor supply store, gave everyone much to dream about.

Heather lent us her four-wheeler the day before we were due to leave. Gary drove us up on the spongy tundra behind the airstrip for a look around.

'What about bear attacks?' I asked worriedly.

Gary chuckled. 'You'll be safe, honey. The bears will be either hibernating or preparing for it now,' he reassured me. 'They'll be high up on the ridges.' That, apparently, was where they preferred to winter over. 'Besides,' he added, 'we will be making too much damned noise to see any animals.' He gave me a reassuring hug.

I was staggered at the rapid change in animal and plant life. There had been a complete change of scenery during these last three weeks. Up at the airstrip the tundra had browned off and was now very boggy. I kept getting off the four-wheeler as we ground down again and again into the saturated and spongy turf.

'Wow, look at that!' I waved my gloved hand out across the village, river and tundra beyond. Gary was busy pushing the bike out of the boggy tundra yet again. The handprint of winter was everywhere. I was reminded again how inconsequential the little village looked in the grand scheme of the great Alaskan wilderness.

On the day we left, there were many messages of God Speed and hope for our safe return. I felt flattered that there was such genuine desire for me to come back. In the short time of my visit I had already made friends.

Gary was more preoccupied. 'I'm worried about leaving the school,' he confided. 'Discipline problems have a tendency to escalate when I'm not here.'

Heavily rugged up in jackets, facemasks, scarves and gloves we boarded the large plane. The ten-seater caravan aircraft would fly us directly out. We sat alongside each other, holding hands through our thick gloves. Earplugs in place, we soared once more out of the village. We both stared down at this landscape that simply took the breath away. Periodically a hand squeeze would alert the other to something through the window. The loud thrumming of the aircraft had an intensely pacifying effect, and Gary was soon asleep. With the cold and the windows fogging up, the view disappeared from sight, so I eventually closed my eyes too.

Our arrival at Anchorage airport was a shock. Noise and traffic hit my senses. The overpowering smell of aircraft fumes. People seemed to be rushing everywhere. There were fast food outlets and lots of white people. I felt like I was in a trance, or coming out of a general anaesthetic and seeing everything sharpen and come into focus as my dreamscape dissolved.

Gary knew his way and after grabbing our bags, he hailed a taxi to the hotel. I wandered alongside, shell shocked at the invasion of this civilisation on my consciousness. I longed to go back to the peace I had left.

A small nod and smile from a native couple in the hotel foyer was reassuring. It was a quiet reminder of a special secret. We knew a land that few had access to. It was a land that held many greater riches and a much gentler way of life than this.

Our parting was much less stressful than the last. We would be back together in about two months. Our meeting was to be in Los Angeles, right before Christmas. As I boarded the Alaskan jet bound for Los Angeles the following day, still trying to hold on to the memories and thoughts of these weeks in the village, I was imagining how I would begin to describe to others what I had experienced.

My thoughts returned to the grey-brown, dusty, wooden buildings of my first week. The softly low Yup'ik voices with their melodic greeting, *Waqaa*, accompanied by shy smiles.

The native people had been a source of warmth and joy in the remote, starkly unforgiving wilderness that was bush Alaska.

Chapter 26

Dawn of the New Millennium

I had arranged to take Kotzman down to Balcutha. We wanted to be there over the millennium. We thought we'd see the dawn of the first millennium from Kaka Beach, where I had spent so many hours with Bel, my little terrier. She could come too.

Over the next few days we took in the sights of Christchurch from the gondola to the beaches. My father even took Kotz for a drive in the MGBGT, and the three came back purring.

'Great car, sir. Thanks for letting me drive.' Kotz was grinning as they unfolded out of the car. Letting him *drive*. Wow! My father was a definite Kotz convert.

We had planned on having Christmas with my family. It was the first Christmas I had had with them for many years. My parents seemed anxious to see as much of Kotzman as they could in the short time he was there.

Kotz was used to having a white Christmas. He had been enthralled at the prospect of a summer Kiwi Christmas.

'I'm cooking lamb for us, dear,' my mother explained, 'but I think I'll do a turkey as well.' At Christmas dinner, Kotz had his first taste of lamb. He said he appreciated the turkey more.

My parents really liked him. I was feeling reassured and quite proud of myself, and I wanted to remind everyone who would listen how sensible I really was emailing this Alaskan stranger. I noticed those around me joining my own mantra, 'What a nice man.' I kept saying smugly to anyone who would listen, 'See, I *told* you he was a nice guy. I *knew* him already!'

In the second week of his stay, I drove Kotzman down to the southernmost tip of New Zealand, to Invercargill and back through South Otago. We drove back on the beautiful coast road. He could not believe that there were so few people on the long golden beaches and it was mid summer. 'The water is very cold,' I explained.

'Does it freeze over?' he asked.

'No. Not cold enough here.'

He didn't seem convinced. I knew the Bering Sea froze in Kotzebue. After picnicking on the beach and getting his toes wet he yelled, 'Boy! Oh wow . . . cold!' I smiled.

We walked back to the car along a track that passed through a dense stand of native trees.

Kotzman remarked, 'You know, Sunshine, this Catlins scenery is very like Southeast Alaska. Like Sitka.' Sitka lay further south on the Canadian latitude. 'You're *sure* there are no wild animals around?' He looked for my nod. 'Seems unbelievable.'

He kept glancing over his shoulder. Kotz was used to being alert for moose and bears. He regaled me on the walks with stories of close encounters.

'You know I'd a great friend who went fishing in the Southeast one day. He placed his catch on the ground beside him. Imagine his surprise when he turned around. There was a bear standing right next to him. No argument there!' He laughed loudly at the memory, still glancing about.

After I had been driving and showing him much of the stunning scenery of the southern end of the island, Kotzman said, 'Sunshine, d'you mind if we stop exploring for a while?' I looked at him in surprise. 'I'm getting giddy with all this scenery and travelling. I need to stop a while. You know I'd rather walk around than drive.'

I was pleased. Even though I had another month's holiday after he left to recuperate, I was also feeling exhausted. We returned to Balclutha.

'My, look at you, little one!' Kotz said to Bel when we arrived home. She ignored me and made straight for him.

'Come on!' He sat and patted his knee. Bel jumped into his lap and lay like a cat with one eye open to check what I thought. I knew Kotz was great with animals, but I did feel a bit hurt. It seemed they had forged a secret pact that excluded me.

We had planned by email what we would do on 31 December 1999. We had decided to take some fish and chips down to Kaka Beach, rig up a bivouac, light a fire and wait for the dawn.

Kotzman's first foray into the fish and chip shop at Balclutha on the eve of the millennium was a sight to behold.

'Hallo there,' he greeted the friendly Asian fish and chip man, who darted me a small smile of recognition. Sometimes when Bel and I headed out to the beach on a Friday night, we stopped off for fish and chips here on the way. Tonight we were alone in the shop. Usually there was a bit of a crowd.

'I'd like to try some of these,' Kotzman gestured broadly at the noticeboard above the fryers. On the board were lists advertising the array of choices. Each choice had an accompanying sketch. Those tourists unfamiliar with the offerings from a New Zealand fish and chip shop could select by picture.

The shopkeeper smiled and nodded. This was good. An American.

'I'll have half a dozen oysters, scallops and maybe a couple of hotdogs.' He turned to me, remarking loudly, 'That's not an American hot dog; that's what we call a corn dog. Hotdogs come in a bun with mustard and ketchup.'

I smiled apologetically at him.

'I'll also have a coupla . . . no, maybe three sausages, ohhh . . . six mussels and two . . . no, four pineapple rings.' He looked pleased with himself. I wondered if he had any idea how much food he was ordering.

'Um, are you getting any fish?' I asked, trying to break through his reverie.

'Oh, yeah. Give me a couple of pieces of that rig and some blue cod too, please.'

'How many, sir?' asked the owner nodding vigorously. We were obviously feeding a large crowd.

'Oh, I dunno, three I think.' The men smiled at each other.

'Don't forget to get some chips,' I mumbled to him. That was my favourite. He could eat the rest. I wanted a piece of blue cod and some chips. My mouth was watering.

'Oh, and as the lady says, some chips – fries we call those.' He laughed aloud again.

The Asian man was smiling and nodding deferentially. He probably thought we had a party on this grand eve of the millennium. It had definitely been worth opening the shop tonight.

'How much ships, sir?'

'Ships?'

'Ships. Yes, sir.' He smiled and nodded a couple more times encouragingly.

Kotz looked at me puzzled.

'Maybe a scoop would do.' I smiled at the man, giving emphasis to the 'would do'. I wanted to let him know we were erring on the cautious size for all those people we would be feeding. I could never come in here again if he thought all that food was just for us.

Kotz and I walked out into the fresh air, Kotz clutching several bundles in his arms.

'Blimey,' I said. 'You'll never eat all that!' Kotz was looking a bit shaken himself. He had three large parcels. It had cost him rather a lot.

'Oh well,' he countered. 'It's a special night. Don't matter!'

We parked in the small car park overlooking Kaka Beach. We would walk about two kilometres along the beach to the camping place. We lugged the food, tarpaulin, blankets and picnic basket between us. We had thermoses, some fruit and snacks, plus the three large parcels of food. Kotz had to make two trips. Bel bounded happily at our ankles. She knew where to go.

We settled by a very large log that I had found on my walks along the beach. I often sat there. Bel was excited as much by the sea as she was by the delicious smell of hot food.

Once Kotz was back, we plonked ourselves down on a picnic blanket and opened the packets. Kotzman looked a little surprised at the vast quantities of food he had ordered.

'Might have ordered too much,' he said, and laughed. I was tucking into my blue cod. 'Mmmmm,' I agreed.

We ended up eating a fraction of it. Kotz tried most and really liked the oysters and fish. I ate my fish and chips, and half a hotdog. I gave the rest of it to Bel. Bel feasted and so did the seagulls.

'Want a cup of tea?' I asked, pulling out the thermos. I was ready for a nice cup of tea.

'No thanks, I'm off to collect some drift wood,' Kotz said, standing up. 'I'll have a coffee later.' He seemed much keener on black coffee than tea, even if it was only instant.

Kotzman spent quite some time collecting long lengths of driftwood. He was making a bivouac against the large log that sheltered us from the prevailing wind. I was impressed. We both then collected lots more wood. There were plenty of beautiful shells. Small paua. I collected those too. It was all very relaxing. We had grown very comfortable now in each other's company.

Kotzman lit a small fire.

'I've been thinking,' I told him. 'See what I've collected?' I showed him my handful of beach treasures. 'Why don't we take small pieces of wood like these, or some shells. We can then name them as some of the old worries and hurts we've had.' We both knew each other's lives intimately from emailing. 'After we've done that we could throw them into the fire. That way we would be burning away those old painful memories. They'll be gone like the old millennium.'

'Good idea.' Kotz went off collecting.

We spent the summer's evening with some very quiet time thinking and talking about our lives to this point. He sipped black coffee while I sipped my tea. It was very familiar territory for us. As we sacrificed small sticks and shells into the flames, we seemed to be burning away our past woes. It felt magical to be with Kotzman awaiting the millennium here on my familiar beach.

Eventually, as the night turned black, we crawled into the shelter. We had added jackets and warm socks to keep out the freezing wind, but we kept a respectful distance apart. Bel was nestled between us. We ended up curled up on the rugs under that billowing bivouac while the sea thundered in. At times it sounded close enough to swamp us.

Kotz nudged me awake while it was still dark. 'Sunshine, dawn is about to break.'

I hadn't slept that well. Too much excitement and food. I had been aware of his closeness. I slid out of the bivouac, shaking out my hair and scanning the horizon. The grey sky was brightening.

'Look,' he said, passing me a mug of tea. He had scratched up the fire and heated up the water. The fire was gently burning. Smoke of the new dawn.

We sat on the sea side of our log, huddled together with our mugs. It was cool but clear. As we watched, the sun slowly stained the grey sky of night with its soft dawning light. I pulled my long skirt on over my long pants. I had brought it especially for this occasion. I stood up barefooted and walked down to the waves. I wanted to welcome the dawn with an ancient Maori waiata.

Standing in the damp sand down by the breakers I was filled with awe at this occasion. Kotzman remained up at our camp and watched. Bel was out already, busy looking for forgotten fish and chips. As the sun tipped the sea's horizon, I began to sing.

On the second of January 2000, Kotzman flew out to Auckland from Dunedin Airport. 'I need to be back in Kotzebue on the third. I'll gain a day back while travelling,' he said. He didn't really need to tell me again, I remembered the details from his emails.

We had been together just over two weeks now and were very comfortable with each other. Because of this familiarity, I was expecting Kotzman to be a bit more forthcoming about what he thought of me. I had really become impressed with him. I was wondering how I would feel about him leaving. I doubted we would ever meet again. It was too far and too expensive.

The whole exercise had proved to me how unimportant first physical impressions could be. Kotz was mostly a quiet man, but he was great socially. He made people feel comfortable easily. He also loved New Zealand. But, I wondered, what did he really think about me?

On the morning of his departure at Dunedin airport, he gave me a quick kiss on my cheek. 'Sunshine, I'll be back,' were his departing words.

Wow, I thought, he is thinking of coming back. I felt forlorn as he crossed the tarmac. He turned and gave a cheery wave before ducking into the plane. I had enjoyed his company. The visit had been a lot better than I had anticipated.

I drove thoughtfully home alone to Bel and Balclutha.

Chapter 27

Homeward Bound

Jet bound for New Zealand, this time with the greenstone necklace that I always wore tucked carefully under my light green jumper – I was determined not to profile as an Irish Terrorist again – I settled down to think. Apart from being singled out for extra security checks, there had been no further problems with the LA police.

On this leg I could now concentrate. I would be returning to Alaska during the January school holidays. Gary and I would be spending a white Christmas in Villa Grove with his mother. I would be missing the New Zealand summer. The thought of resigning and then once more packing and moving, after having been settled in New Zealand for a short three years, had been intimidating. Now I knew I just had to get on with it. I pulled out my list of things to do.

Jenny met me at the airport and took me to my parents' place. We sat around talking about the trip and my decision.

'I can see the sense in it,' my father reluctantly agreed. 'Sometimes these moves offer the best opportunities for the future.'

My parents had decided that they would take Bel. She had stayed with them while I had been away, and seemed settled and happy in their company. I was grateful, as this meant we could keep her. It would be one less loss for Ella.

I drove back through the soft green hills to Balclutha the following day. I would need to call the Immigration Department immediately and find out what I needed to do before leaving for Alaska again. I also had to organise my teaching papers to send to California for verification and assessment for teaching in the United States. I was anxious to get back to Balclutha and get started on all of this. I had limited time to get everything done.

My first stop back had been Mr Mark. 'So you're going back to live there, Emma?' He smiled. It crossed my mind that he and Gary had set up the whole plan between them. 'We will be very sorry to lose you.' He pulled a sad face. 'But I reckon you are doing the right thing.' Grinning mischievously he added, 'Maybe I'll even visit!'

After my return to Balclutha, the local South Otago Country Women's Institute asked me to come back and give another talk about Alaska.

'You know what it's like when these Americans come here,' I started the evening by saying. Small smiles flitted across the faces near me. 'You know when they say everything is bigger and wider and more grandiose over there?' I gestured widely with my arms. There was laughter and loud assenting murmurs. Some turned and nodded in agreement to each other. 'Well,' I paused for maximum effect, 'I am here to tell you that it *is*!' Huge laughter. I was off to a great start.

What remained of the year seemed to race very quickly to an end. There was so much to do. I was still working full time. In order to make LA before Christmas, I would be leaving Balclutha as soon as school finished. It meant working late into the nights after long school days. At the end of term I would drive back up to Christchurch with Bel. Dad said he'd sell my car for me.

Mr Mark organised a large afternoon tea and farewell for me in the staff room the last week of school. Summer had arrived. Already the temperature was soaring and the hills were starting to brown off. There, amongst friends and laughter, I received a first aid box of 'Things to help you when you get to Alaska'. It contained a toothpick, one band aid, duct tape, an ice tray to 'make use of what is around you', and a mock-up 'one way ticket back'. I was also given a beautiful book on the South Otago countryside.

I packed in a dream. It had seemed such a short time ago when I had arrived, unpacked and set up. Now here I was leaving again. How on earth had *that* happened?

I knew the reasons for going. I thought about them constantly. Apart from the stunning beauty and draw of the bush Alaska I had experienced, it was all back to money and financial security again. Gary and I were both trying to build a stronger financial base. The Sydney apartment was rolling along. I had had a change of tenants and was now able to increase the rent. I no longer had to top up mortgage repayments.

Gary needed five more years and he would be vested in the Alaska Teachers' Retirement Scheme. That would mean ongoing financial support in retirement wherever in the world he lived. We could save much more money if we were both living in Alaska together. If I could get a job teaching we might be able to manage on my wage and save his. The money would give us a financial base to build a future upon. Maybe we could even save enough to buy a house in New Zealand.

My great plan of each of us staying and working at opposite ends of the world to the other had had two fatal flaws. The first was the expense. It was extremely expensive flying all that way twice a year. Lots of savings lost there. The second was the main flaw in my argument. Intellectually and theoretically it had made sense, but I had omitted to consider the emotional impact of the plan. We had missed each other terribly.

If I moved to Alaska with Gary, not only could we support each other, we could also enjoy a huge adventure together. Having visited Alaska, I felt that was now an extremely exciting idea. Experience had pulled up the anchor on my plan. I was about to sail into the great unknown.

As far as Ella was concerned, we could fly her out to see us in Alaska. She seemed quite enchanted with the idea. A plane trip to see me was a plane trip. She understood well the idea of developing a stronger financial base.

In the end I stored most of my precious furniture and sentimental keepsakes at a local storage centre. I also mailed some boxes out to Pilot Station. Postage was over $100 per small box, so I had not sent much. I'd stuffed in some plastic flowers though. I had never thought that I would be buying plastic flowers. They were light in weight, filled up odd spaces, and would be reminiscent of the garden colours of home.

I sold off furniture and things that I would not need from my teacher flat. I'd bought a large dresser at my favourite antique shop in Milton a week before I left. It looked perfect to display all those objects I knew I would be bringing back to New Zealand one day in the future. I just had to come back. Anyway I had promised Gary we would.

I couldn't bring myself to sell my refuge at Measly Beach. It had provided such a wonderful interlude in my life. 'Please come and use the place,' I urged friends and family. I told them where the key was hidden. 'I know it can be cold and blustery and a long way to get to. But it is lovely when you get the fire going.'

Kotzman had told me he was colder out there than in the Arctic Circle. But I couldn't bear to sell it. I would think more about the practicality of keeping it later. I'd do that from the distance of Alaska and from within Gary's arms.

Chapter 28

A New Year's Surprise

Kotzman emailed as soon as he returned to Kotzebue. 'Got back okay, Sunshine. My, I miss you already.' My heart lurched. He was missing me too! I now had a much clearer picture of him. I could picture him writing.

'Weather here is freezing. Know the first thing I did? I made some hedges out of snow!' I laughed out loud. Christchurch must really be on his mind.

'Mato's fine,' he chatted on. 'Beth did a good job in minding him.' His native secretary Beth was married to the school's groundsman. They knew Mato well. Kotz had trusted them to keep Mato from some of the wild dogs in the village. Most of the dogs there were half wolves. 'Mind you, he has been peeing on the hedges and they are starting to collapse in places, LOL.' I could just picture it all. 'How's Clutha? Bel?'

What could I say? It was the middle of the summer holidays and I was actually feeling a little forlorn. After the explosion and excitement of Kotzman's visit, the world now seemed a bit dull. Bel plodded along dutifully on our walks. We were coming home to the silly old computer. Having now met, emailing was definitely not the satisfying communication it had been before. Nothing like the real thing.

'We're fine,' I wrote. I couldn't seem to get up much enthusiasm for emailing.

In Kotzebue, Kotz was heading into the second semester. It was still pitch dark most of the time. Deep snow everywhere. He was very busy.

In contrast, my days were long and lazy. I had bought myself a bike from the local bike shop. Carol, my teacher neighbour and I had been going out biking together. It could be quite windy, but the exercise distracted me and kept me going. I would come home with late summer flowers in the basket. Flowers that had been growing by the side of the road.

Several weeks into his second semester Kotz wrote, 'How would you feel if I came back at the end of my school year? I'm thinking of taking a year's sabbatical.' He thought he might write a paper on the local Maori pre-school – the kohanga reo.

This time there was no hesitation. 'Oh, yes! Of course! That'd be absolutely great,' I responded. 'He's coming back!' I shouted to Bel who was lying at my feet. I thought she looked really pleased.

Kotzman wanted me to find him a small place locally that he could rent. It would give us time to get to know each other properly, like people usually did. Besides, really we hadn't even had a proper date. It would be great to maybe go through a romantic ritual.

I was excited. Now I had a mission. I had to find a place. First I wanted to tell my family and close friends.

'That's lovely, dear,' said my mother, 'but where will he stay?'

Dad said, 'Mm-hm' in a non-committal sort of a way.

'Great!' rejoiced Jenny, 'I'll get him to help me with Honey pulling on the lead.'

Ella arrived at Dunedin airport from Sydney for the Easter break. I took Bel in the car to the airport to greet her, and they were both very excited to see each other. Ella thought the flat was cute, but very rural.

We chatted into the night. 'Mum,' she said looking perplexed, 'when do I get to meet this man everyone's telling me about?'

'Mmm,' I responded. 'You do need to meet him too.' I was thinking aloud. 'What do you think of the idea of him flying back to New Zealand via Sydney?'

'That'd be good,' she reflected. 'Do you think he would do that?'

'Yes, I think he would.' I was thinking ahead. 'You know, maybe in July, when I am over, I could book him into that backpackers I stay at around the corner from you.'

'Yeah.' She looked thoughtful. 'You really think I'll like him?'

'I think you will.' I smiled. 'He'll have to meet Paratai as well.' We both laughed, me more nervously than her. Oh yeah, he definitely would need to do that.

My holidays raced along. School started again. In between my studies and my daily travels I started looking around. I was searching for a small holiday home, or crib, as they were known down in South Otago. A place that Kotzman could rent for several months. Trouble was most people wanted their places back over the summer.

One day I received an excited call from the kuia Mona at work. I had told her I was looking for something. 'Kia ora, Emma. I have found just the right place for you out here near where we live. Come out for tea and have a look.'

'Fantastic!' I was excited. Mona lived out on the coast on a farm overlooking the sea. I had been out to visit her and her husband Bob late in the holidays. It was private and spectacular out there. Just the sort of place Kotzman would love.

'I'll let the owners know you're coming late afternoon.' She hung up.

I drove straight out there after work. Measly Beach was a 40-minute drive north and out along the coast. The road was bumpy and every mile the words of 'Country road, take me home,' kept playing over in my head.

I found the crib she described, but with a 'For Sale' sign up. I walked up the paddock to the front door. The crib was settled against a hill. One side faced the country road, the other the sea. I could smell fresh salt air and feel chilling wind. The owners were there. They were expecting me. I knocked on the door.

'Come in,' they called. I walked into a small kitchen combined with a dining area and lounge. The rooms were basked in the late afternoon sun. An elderly couple sat on the couch. A large old stove stood at one end, a bedroom was at the other. Even inside I could hear the waves crashing onto the beach.

'We want to sell it,' the man spoke. 'We're moving back up north.'

'How much?' I gulped. I wasn't sure I wanted to be *buying* any more properties.

'Eight thousand dollars.' Eight thousand dollars? Was he serious? 'It is on leased land,' he added. He searched my face for an answer. 'Comes completely furnished.'

'I'll buy it,' I said immediately. We shook hands. They looked pleased.

'Come and look around,' he said.

There was another small detached bedroom, an outside toilet and enclosed shower. It was rustic, but perfect. I was thrilled.

I drove over to Mona's and told her the news. She was as excited as I was. 'It's on our land, you know,' she said with a grin. I didn't know. But that was even better.

She would make sure I was okay.

After dinner with Mona, I couldn't wait to get home and email Kotzman. First, though, I needed to call my parents.

'Guess what,' I wrote to Kotzman online later, 'I've bought me a little holiday house out by the beach.'

'Really!' Kotz responded. He was taken aback that I had bought another property. 'Can you afford to?' He knew money was tight. Especially when I had told him that topping up mortgage repayments in Sydney was an ongoing strain for me.

'Yes, I can afford to.'

Go on, I thought, ask me how much.

'How much?'

'Eight thousand dollars.' I looked at the written amount. I still couldn't believe how cheap it was.

'You're serious?'

'I sure am. It's on leased land. Belongs to the kuia Mona and her husband.'

'Oh, wow!'

'It's perfect. I can go out there in the weekends in the meantime. My own little escape.'

Kotzman was as excited as I was. 'Can you send me some pics? When I stay there I'll pay the rent, of course.' Kotz was anxious not to put any financial burden on me. Raising two children alone, he knew about financial struggle. We'd discussed how much renting a crib would be for him.

'Mum and Dad have offered to loan me the money,' I wrote. 'I'll pay them back a little at a time.' I had already paid back my car quite quickly. They liked the idea of a retreat by the sea, especially my mother. They knew that Kotzman was coming back and could live out there. I had told them I knew he would be happy to pay rent.

'I'm going to call it Kotahitanga,' I wrote.

'Kotahitanga?'

'That is what I have named it. It means as one.' I couldn't stop grinning.

As soon as the sale document was signed I took Bel out to Kotahitanga for the weekend. I needed to take some pictures for Kotz and to explore.

Walking back in there I was thrilled. It was everything I had dreamed of as a holiday home, and as it came fully furnished, I didn't need to buy one thing. Even linen and blankets were left.

The front of the property faced the road, the back nestled against a large sand hill. A track took you down to the beach. The beach was perfect. Long uninterrupted stretches of golden sand where I could walk with Bel for miles. If I lit the stove the little house would be cosy by the time I got back, I thought. I could cook on the top of the stove, or in the electric oven. There was a small detached sleep-out and an outside toilet, all under cover. A pergola porch connected the rooms and would keep you dry. I was overjoyed with my purchase.

Bob, Mona's pakeha husband, wandered over while I was exploring. Bob took out a rollup cigarette and looked at the large sand hill behind the property. The dining room window view looked directly into the hill, which was about three metres away.

'Blocks your view a bit, that hill,' he spoke through his teeth as he puffed.

'Yes it does, but I can get all the views I like by sitting up there.' I pointed to the bank behind the house where a little seat was nestled looking out to sea. 'It's a lovely walk down the track to the beach.' I grinned happily at him.

Bob drew on his cigarette slowly.

'We could take that out.' He nodded at the hill.

I gawped at him, incredulous. How could he take out a sand hill? Where would he put the sand? Was he serious?

'Got a back hoe over at the farm this week,' he gestured with his head. 'Want it gone?' He nodded at the hill.

'I can't afford that. Anyway, where could you put all that sand?' I still thought he was joking.

'Down the other side of the hill.' He flipped his head again and looked serious. 'No charge. No worries. Easy.'

How could he just take a sand hill and drop it off the other side down the bank?

'You can't do that.'

He took out his cigarette and grinned at me. 'Why not, I own the hill . . . and the stream.'

I had no argument for that.

When I drove back out there the following Friday it was as if a large bite had been taken out of the back of the property. From my dining-room window I could now see all the way out to sea. It was spectacular. Bob wandered over when he saw my car.

'Waddya think?' He looked pleased.

'Oh Bob, it is amazing! Thank you!'

He gave me a wry grin. I decided to try a rollup too. Even though I didn't smoke, it was the least I could do. We sat on the top of the bank and looked down at his handiwork.

'I reckon you're gonna need some topsoil, to stop that sand flying away from the cut,' he added thoughtfully, lighting my wreck of a cigarette. 'I can get you some of that.'

I wasn't arguing. If he could take out a sand hill, I knew he could get me some topsoil. What I didn't reckon on, though, was just how much.

The next day a 40-tonne truck backed up to the top of the hill overlooking the cut. The driver dropped off a huge load of beautiful rich clumps of topsoil with luscious green Otago grass. Most of the sods tumbled down and overturned, and they lay there in a huge pile, many upside down. I was very worried that the grass would die like that. I didn't want to waste it. I needed to move it quickly.

I had a barrow, so all day I loaded it with sods and carted it across to the far cut face of sand. Sod by sod I started to build a wall of grass. Bel lay in the sun watching.

I imagined myself building a pyramid. I placed the first long row along the base of the hill, approximately 20 large clumps of turf. I stamped them down with my gumboots. Then I worked on the row above, carefully placing them hard down on the row below so they wouldn't slip. Each row was slightly shorter than the one below.

Slowly I worked my way up the hill. It was satisfying using up all this beautiful dirt and rebuilding a grass wall that would stand for ages. By the end of the day I was finished. I was also totally exhausted.

I was lying flat out on my back on the bed, feet on the floor and gumboots still on, when I heard the sound of a large truck. I struggled up and opened the back door. Standing on the brim of the hill where the first load had been dropped were three men. One of them was Bob. I heard someone swear.

'Look at *that*!' Bob said. 'She's a worker all right!' I waved at them from the backdoor. I felt proud, even though it was an effort to stand upright. Suddenly there was a huge rumble, and another load tumbled down the hill. I now had enough for the other side.

Chapter 29

Mid-Winter in Pilot Station

Our return to Pilot Station was in mid January, mid winter. Gary and I had spent a wonderfully white Christmas in the Mid West town of Villa Grove with Gary's mother, sister and her family. It had been freezing. The screen on my digital camera had frozen black in the severe cold. From then on any photos were a point and shoot and hope I got what I wanted.

I wanted to capture the fairy lights that decorated the houses, just like the many Christmas cards I had seen over the years. Villa Grove was very pretty in the snow.

We had stayed with Gary's mother in the small family home. We had been equally thrilled to finally meet each other. It was as if we had known each other all our lives.

Before leaving Villa Grove we were invited to attend a service there at the local church. Special prayers from the community were made before our journey back to Alaska and, as someone put it, 'off the end of the world'. It made me realise again the enormity of this return to the wilderness. I knew this long journey back out to seclusion and isolation. I could not wait.

This time we took a jet from Anchorage to Bethel, a hub city of about 6000. Bethel was the main port on the Kuskokwim River on the Yukon/Kuskokwim Delta. Because of its geographic position, Bethel was often referred to as the 'underarm of Alaska'. This was also a wry reference to its layout over marshy tundra. I remembered Bethel as the place where Gary had ordered the milk and potatoes for my first visit.

The jet ride to Bethel was terrifying. I gathered the flight attendants knew what was coming when they immediately took away the juice they had just served. 'Please fold away your trays, as the flight might be bumpy,' they announced cheerfully over the intercom. They were already strapped firmly into their dickie seats.

We had undergone a de-icing exercise at Anchorage airport. I had watched the process through the small aircraft windows. Our plane had been sprayed with a pink chemical at high pressure, while we waited onboard. This procedure stopped ice forming on critical parts of the plane, such as the wings, flaps and fuselage. In the dead black night those fire hoses spraying us carefully and methodically under high pressure looked like serious business. It was sobering.

As the jet now climbed into the blackness, I could see the snow swirling past the windows in never-ending flurries, as if escaping from a hole in a giant feather quilt. Nothing appeared to settle on the wings, but the large plane trembled and shook in the exertion of staying on track. The fact that it seemed to be tossed around so easily was extremely unnerving.

I knew Gary was worried about me. The normally placid traveller in me had undergone a metamorphosis. I had turned into an arm gripping, jaw clenching woman. He tried to allay my fears by describing far more harrowing flights he had had in the past, but that made me sink lower in my chair. I placed my feet wide and strong on the floor rather like a Danish-designed armchair I had seen once.

The jet then went through motions such as 'Let's wave our wings at friends on the ground, even though it's pitch dark and a blizzard to boot'. It then followed with 'Let's dive down lower and see if we can see them', and then 'Let's turn off the engines and try bungee jumping'.

The pilot's voice finally came over the intercom with the understatement of the year. 'This is your pilot letting you know we are likely to experience some turbulence.'

Does he not count *this?* I thought. 'We have been told that when we get to Bethel, there is a back log of planes waiting to land.' Why? Are they hovering over others that have crashed? 'And as fourth in the queue we will have to circle for an extra 20 minutes or more.' Horror, not *more* of this. 'But do not worry, we have 90 minutes worth of fuel.'

I was wishing he had not said that. I would now be attempting to check my watch to see how many minutes left before certain doom. Luckily I could not even read my watch as we were shaking and vibrating so much.

Eventually we landed. It was with huge relief that I could now resume friendly chatter with Gary. He had witnessed a woman in the throes of terror for much of the ride. My only conversation throughout had been a series of grunts and rolling of the eyes.

I had been warned that there were no undercover passageways when disembarking in Bethel. It was essential we were dressed ready for the weather when the plane doors opened. Gloves, hats and scarves as well as heavy jackets were the apparel for all.

Before flying out, Gary and I had spent two days shopping in Anchorage, buying parkas, coveralls, facemasks, gloves and heavy duty warm boots. The cumbersome Arctic boots allowed the wearer warm feet at minus 80 degrees. They would be good on the snow machine. I was rather pleased with my purchase of walking boots. The dark grey boots were on special and much more elegant than the clumpy ones I had seen. They were calf high with a shaped top, and like *mukluks*, the reindeer or sealskin boots traditionally worn by the Alaskan native people, they were decorated with grey fur. We also purchased ice cleats, spikes attachable under the shoes by elastic bands over the top.

The large quantities of groceries we had bought had been packed into 20-litre plastic tubs. Gary had mailed everything back to us at Pilot Station at the post office in Anchorage. The post office by the airport was always open 24 hours for bush shoppers. We were kitted out, stored up and ready for winter.

However, it was time to disembark and I could not find my gloves. We searched the overhead bins, pockets in front. Gary got down on the floor and checked under the seats, nothing.

Gary lent me his gloves. My legs were very unsteady. He helped me climb down the stairs and pick my way across the snowy tarmac. I just could not get my woolly hat to pull down over my ears. It had before the flight. It now appeared my head must have billowed out in terror during this ordeal. As we entered the airport I pulled off my hat.

'Here they are!' I cried with relief. My gloves had been cleverly placed inside the hat for safekeeping. Gary roared with laughter and I chuckled weakly along. It was an unforgettable reminder of the inability to think clearly when the mind was preoccupied with survival.

Walking into the terminal was like walking into Father Christmas's toy factory staffed by the elves. Everywhere there was action. Small people with beaming pink cheeks, furs, mittens, boots, bags and boxes. There was chatting and greeting, and great excitement. Several of the locals from Pilot Station recognised us and came over to hug us. It felt like a real home-coming. I couldn't decide if I was more relieved to be back on terra firma, or back in this special world again.

We stayed at a local bed and breakfast in Bethel overnight. Bethel was blanketed in deep white snow. The snow was piled so high on the road verges it looked as if the houses were sinking into the depths.

Our flight back to Pilot Station was to leave early the following afternoon. I dressed in all my new warm clothing for this last flight. Our point of departure was a terminal dedicated to bush flights. The small rectangular room was packed with people in winter gear. The native women now wore furs under their *quspuks*. I admired again the utility of their way of dressing. Rabbit pelts were stitched together with the fur lying against the skin for warmth. The *quspuk* was then simply dropped over the top. Wolverine fur that did not freeze circled the hood. More decorative furs like white or red fox appeared at neck, wrist and hem. Furs were a symbol of standing in the native communities.

At this terminal, departure times had nothing to do with the published times. You would leave when the quota of passengers was reached and when the weather settled enough for a pilot to risk flying there. Today the planes were leaving early, late or not at all.

The departure announcement was simple. A pilot would walk into the crowd that would suddenly be stilled with anticipation. With clipboard in hand the pilot, always male, would call a village destination. Passengers would quickly and quietly gather all their belongings together. This included the children who were scattered throughout the room. As the passengers formed a ragged queue by the door, the pilot would say each name and check them off. No one ever seemed to be missing. Headscarves and gloves would be slipped on and the passengers would lumber out into the freezing atmosphere. The group would climb onto one of the many tiny bush planes sitting out on the tarmac. The propeller would start, then the plane would do a quick turn onto the icy runway and be gone. The whole procedure took no more than five minutes. Time was critical.

After a four-hour wait the pilot called us for Tutalgaq. As we flew out of Bethel, we were looking down now on pristine white everywhere, as if this world had been dusted heavily with icing sugar. We suddenly dropped and landed at Pilot Station, skidding on the ice strip that had been cleared of snow by a grader. It amazed me how the snow and ice on the ground did not have the ability to stop flights landing and taking off. Everyone was unrecognisable, covered completely from top to toe. We recognised James only by the school truck. He dropped us home.

'Great to see you both again. Been busy since you left. We had a break-in of the school food-storage area last night. One of the kids.' Gary and James discussed the break-in briefly. James had caught the culprit. Apparently the state trooper was arriving the following day. He would drive his car along the frozen Yukon River and be staying with us.

We had come back to no radio, no newspaper, TV when it worked, phone when it worked and the post office when it was open. We now had a VHF radio base at home, tuned into the local radio band. Gary could hear when the planes were landing for the winter tournaments. He would need to transport the students back and forth to school.

He turned on the new VHF. Tuning into the local radio band I heard a girl's voice, 'Mum, come pick me up?'

Maybe this world was not so different after all.

Chapter 30

Another Visit Down Under

When Kotzman returned to Alaska after his first trip to New Zealand, he had decided to resign his principalship at the end of the school year. He would take one year's sabbatical leave and then decide what to do. Maybe he would be able to find work in New Zealand. First he wanted to pay off his final debt for his doctorate degree and save for this trip back. During his time in New Zealand, he wanted to be totally financially independent from me.

Kotzman started sending me boxes: artefacts of his time in Alaska; his teaching manuals and personal keepsakes. These were exciting mail delivery days in Balclutha.

'Sunshine, no worries about the rent for Kotahitanga,' he wrote. 'It will help you pay off your parents' loan quickly.' I knew his most difficult decision had been about Mato. At nine years of age Mato was an old dog and would not survive the imposed quarantine that bringing him to New Zealand would require. Kotz had spent a week checking that out. His secretary, Beth, and her husband loved Mato. They offered to mind him. They were moving out to Palmer, closer to civilisation. They would be back on the coveted Alaskan road system. They owned a small log cabin in the woods there, where there were streams and large wooded areas for Mato to run. Beth also offered to store some of Kotz's things.

Kotzman would be coming to New Zealand initially on a three-month visitor's visa. During this time he would apply for a work permit.

Nothing was definite. We would take it from there. This arrangement softened the reality of Kotzman leaving Mato. I knew how hard it all was.

'Jared is resigning too,' Kotz wrote shortly after. Jared was Kotz's deputy. Kotz's leaving had spurred Jared's decision. 'He doesn't want to be here with me gone.'

'Wow, the school is really going to notice you both leaving.'

'Yep. He wants to try for a principal's job. He'll look for somewhere smaller to work.'

When the time came, saying farewell to Elmer, the students, parents and staff had been much more difficult than Kotz had expected. He had been in Kotzebue three years. On his last morning the student council decorated his office as a surprise. Blue and gold streamers and dozens of balloons greeted him when he opened his door that last morning. 'Farewell, Doc, we'll miss you,' was written on the banner that draped his desk.

Elmer presented him with a jade and ivory clock he had made especially. 'Time,' he said, 'to remember to come back.'

'You know, Sunshine,' Kotzman wrote. 'The only way I can get through all this is thinking about New Zealand.'

Kotzman had decided to fly home and spend some time with his mother over the northern summer. I would be very busy with work and assignments, and would appreciate the lack of distractions. I had booked to go to Sydney late July in my winter holidays and see Ella. I would be back early August.

'I'll hang out with Mom and have some down time. I'll stay with her for a few weeks over the summer holidays,' Kotz had said.

His mother was in her late eighties, and he couldn't be sure how long she would live. He loved her deeply. She was a woman who had always encouraged her children to make their own decisions. She had moved in with him after Kotz's father died. It was at a time when Kotz's children were still small. His mother had helped him for three years with his young family.

Apparently Kotz's mother celebrated the move to New Zealand. 'She tells me she is very happy for me because she knows I am very happy,' Kotz explained.

He would stay with his mother till early August. The weather would be very hot in the States by then. There was no email contact from his mother's house. We agreed he would dedicate his time to his mother and he would call me once a week.

He had made arrangements to fly out of the States and through Australia. Kotz had yet to meet Ella.

Ella called me one Saturday night. 'This guy better be pretty amazing,' she said with caution in her voice. 'He sounds like he thinks he is moving in with you.'

Ella wanted to check him out for herself, and so did my ex-husband, Rick. I knew that Paratai also wanted to meet him. That was going to be interesting. I sent both Kotz and Ella photos of each other.

On the afternoon of Kotz's arrival in Sydney, Ella took a bus out to the airport. She decided to meet Kotzman there. 'I'll watch him walk through the airport doors at Sydney, Mum.' Just like I had in Christchurch, I thought. 'Besides, I don't want him to get lost.'

'And you know what he looks like?' I checked.

'Yeah, I know.' She had seen photos.

As it happened, she missed him completely. He spotted her, and quietly came around the crowd and approached her from behind. She was standing near the rail watching each passenger carefully as they walked out through the sliding doors.

'Ella?' He asked. She spun around.

'Oh! There you are!' She laughed, embarrassed that she'd missed him. She could see it was definitely Kotzman.

I was surprised to receive a call that night from Kotzman and Ella.

They rang me together from the airport to report they had found each other. They both sounded equally excited.

'That's a relief,' I said. One down, two to go.

Rick had given Ella dress-circle seats for her and Kotz to the Buddy Holly show. Rick was performing as Sam Cooke in the show that night. Ella and Kotzman got up and danced with the audience in the aisles. They had a ball. They hit it off just as I thought they might. After the show the two men met.

'Hi there, you must be Rick,' said Kotz. He was amazed how much alike Rick and Ella looked. 'Loved the show. You were great!'

'Thanks,' said my ex. 'Shall we get a drink?'

That night, while walking back from a wine bar they'd visited with Ella, my ex asked Kotz if he had a lift to the airport for his early morning flight two days later.

'I need to be there at six in the morning,' Kotzman told him. 'I'm getting the shuttle.'

'No, man. I'll pick you up at 5:30am, no worries. I insist.' He continued, 'You know, I'm not supposed to, but I really like you.' He grinned sheepishly.

'I know,' smiled Kotzman, 'I feel the same.' They strolled along peaceably with each other.

Kotzman was worried about meeting Paratai. He knew that Paratai had guarded me fiercely from any male interest. 'He's useless,' she would whisper to me. Or, 'That one'll just make you miserable, darling.' Her favourite phrase had been, 'Just you wait, you'll know the right one when he comes along.'

Paratai was anxious to meet this man she had heard so much about. This important meeting was scheduled for 2pm the following afternoon.

Kotzman was waiting in the small café courtyard in Darlinghurst when Paratai arrived. He was extremely nervous. He recognised Paratai immediately; she looked exactly as I had described her. 'Small, slim, smiley face with glasses. She has grey hair and will be carrying her kete, her traditional woven flax basket.'

Paratai was wearing a black suit and small red hat. 'Kia ora,' she said when she saw him. She reached up and gave him a kiss on the cheek. Kotz responded. He had stood and pulled out a chair for her.

'Tena koe,' he slowly sounded out the words he had been practising. Paratai smiled, pleased. That was good. He had made an effort to greet her correctly. He had even used a special greeting of respect to her. This was a good sign.

The meeting passed comfortably. He told me later that he felt like he was being interviewed, but it was a comfortable interview. They had got along well. I knew them both well, so that was not a surprise.

Kotzman spent the remainder of his last day exploring Sydney. He visited Ella and went to Bondi Beach. He called me that evening.

'Getting anxious to get to Balclutha now, Sunshine. I think I've passed the tests.' He sounded tired but happy. He was ready for New Zealand.

The following morning my ex collected him and took him to the airport. They carried the bags in together, chatting like old friends.

'Thanks,' said Kotzman when they reached the check-in counter for New Zealand. 'Would you care to join me for some breakfast?'

'No, man, I better get back. I need some sleep before the gig tonight.' They shook hands and Rick walked off. He got as far as the end of the room, then turned around and headed back to Kotz. Kotzman had just finished the check-in process.

'You know,' he said, 'a coffee would be great.'

Meanwhile, Paratai had caught the early morning train across town to the airport. She wanted to surprise Kotz and be there to farewell him. She also had some gifts for me, along with a sealed envelope containing a note. 'Express Delivery' was written neatly across the front.

When I rang her several days later to thank her for the gifts and to hear more about their meeting, she was still bubbly with excitement and laughter.

'Oh, darling,' she said with a chuckle, 'I arrived at the airport first thing in the morning as a surprise. I turned the corner and saw both of your men sitting having coffee together. It was *me* that was surprised. So, darling, I just sat down and joined them.'

That *was* funny. I could just picture seeing them sitting there – a Maori elder, a white American and an African American. All had been strangers two days earlier. Now they were chatting away over breakfast coffee together very early on a Sydney morning.

Paratai's note, decorated with a smiley-face, simply said, 'See, it was worth waiting.'

Chapter 31

Potlatch Pride

The morning after our return to Pilot Station, I looked out of our lounge room window. Pure white snow draped every upright and horizontal thing. The joy I had witnessed at Bethel on the faces of the locals was a direct result of very heavy snowfalls. They had begun two weeks earlier. This idyllic once-peaceful world was now continuously punctuated with the scream of snow-machine engines. I had heard them deep into the night. With speeds that must have broken the Arctic sound barrier, they had raced each other up and down the track that went right past our front door. Boy racers.

As was true of my earlier visit in the autumn, water problems in the apartment and the village continued. 'Honey, I have some bad news,' Gary announced later that day.

'Yeah?' I wondered what was coming.

'Apparently there's a leak in the city's water supply,' he announced. 'We'll be getting this sporadic water delivery now until spring.'

'Spring!' That was at least three months away according to local knowledge.

'Well, by then the snow will melt. The leaks can then be uncovered and fixed.'

'Blimey!'

The lack of regular water supply certainly made for interesting living. One day in my first week back I had noticed enough water pressure to force water out of the shower spout. With lightening speed I had removed my clothes, determined to get my hair washed while I could. Alas, after I had shampooed my hair with cleanliness fervour, the showerhead decided to stop delivering water at all. For the first time in my life I had found myself crouching stark naked and cold on the floor of the bathtub trying to get my head under the bath faucet. It took half an hour to remove all traces of shampoo from my head by attempting to catch those three warm dribbles per minute. My body was frozen.

The weather continued to amaze me in its changeability. Temperatures now varied between zero and minus 14 degrees Celsius. A day could start out clear and innocent, but within an hour there could be whiteout conditions. Later still, it might either clear completely or a blizzard might be brewing.

During a blizzard the snow blew horizontally past the windows. The window was rather like a large television screen. I watched it from the warmth and luxury of the apartment. The storm blew in tiny flakes for hour after hour, and depending on the wind direction, different parts of the buildings were slowly buried. As soon as the storm stopped, the snow machines would start up again. The new snow made the journey soft and luxurious. Well, Gary told me it did. I preferred to remain indoors. I had to study again.

We had our first potlatch the following week. I wanted to get out of the apartment and go. I had been presented with a new *quspuk* made by Mary's mother, and it fitted perfectly; so I would wear that. I was excited to see the ancient cultural practices again in this modern context.

Two of our local boys were 'coming out'. This was rather like debutantes being presented to society. The difference was that the boys were young – five and six years of age. The boys' families would present them to our village and the surrounding villages. The event was the talk of the school. I asked Gary about it.

'Well, sweetheart, there's gonna be about 300 visitors coming.' He opened his eyes wide to show how impressed he was. 'They're travelling in by snow machine.' The snow now meant more visitors could travel. 'There're also bush plane flights comin' in from St Mary's, Marshall, Kotlik *and* Russian Mission.' Russian Mission was a village 84 kilometres up river from us. Some would be travelling by snow machine from there.

'The boys've been given Yup'ik Eskimo names in the memory of elders who have recently died.'

'Why?'

'It's considered an honour to live on like a wise one remembered. That family then becomes responsible for you as well. You become part of their family.'

'Oh wow.' I liked that idea. It sounded like a great way to celebrate loved ones. I knew there was also a practice here similar to the Maori 'whangai' custom – giving away or adopting out babies to other members of the family, as Maori often did. Sometimes it was more economical for another branch of the family to provide the food and clothing. That way the children would not suffer deprivation in a very large family, but would still retain family links. This meant that no one went without. It seemed that families could interchange quite readily.

The event was being held at the Culture Centre. The day before the event, Gary took along our gifts. He described what he'd seen at lunchtime.

'They've piled everything up in large heaps on the floor. I put down the baseball caps and army gloves on the pile. Others have given practical gifts like toilet paper, shovels and buckets. Once all the gifts are received they'll be stored upstairs in the Cultural Centre.'

'What happens to them all? Is it for the family?'

'No, it's then shared out amongst the local villagers. Everyone gets something to remember the occasion by. That'll happen the next night during continuing celebrations. The time when the Eskimo dancing starts.'

I had been told that potlatches were waning in their occurrence because of the enormous amount of work and preparation families had to do for the event. The boys' parents had to give out many gifts during the ceremony. They also had to catch and prepare food for the feasting. All sorts of delicacies would be expected. *Muktuk*, the delicate whale blubber, would be sent from relatives further north in exchange for local moose. *Akutaq*, Eskimo ice cream made the traditional way, meant deer had to be caught and prepared. Seal oil would be needed for dipping the food. There would be beaver, walrus, moose, hares, fox, fowl and fish. The smoked salmon would have been prepared over the previous summer. That was why there was often a delay in 'coming out'. It could be an expensive and time-consuming business.

On the first night of celebrations, the Cultural Centre was packed. This night only the Pilot Station people danced. Both small boys joined in. They accompanied the elders dancing.

I was amazed at the skill of the small boys. They were immaculately dressed in their *quspuks* especially made for the event. Their hair had been cut in a basin cut. It shone and glistened shiny black in the soft light. They were wearing beautiful skin *mukluks*. The skin boots had been hand-made for them for this occasion. Their dancing and demeanour was impeccable. They had been coached and coached for the event. They represented not only their illustrious namesake, but also their entire family and the village.

Each of their dances was quite long, lasting up to ten minutes. We watched the boys each perform in eight dances. They held their circular feather fans proudly, kneeling in the front of the women as the men sometimes did. They moved gracefully in time with the drums and the wailing, becoming lost in the emotion and movement. This caused great delight in the crowd, who cheered and clapped for them.

On the first night of celebrations, I sat on the front benches by the door of the centre, where Heather and I had sat before. By 7pm the place was full to bursting.

I sat next to a very old Eskimo woman from Russian Mission.

'*Waqaa*,' I said, smiling at her.

'*Waqaa*,' she replied, nodding at me and smiling.

'Many people,' I continued, gesturing to the crowd.

'I say Eskimo,' she said very slowly, as if she were practicing the sounds. I nodded and smiled again. She was about four foot tall and looked very old. Many of the elders were extremely short. I had been told that the smaller stature allowed for better heat retention. Many of the elders reached great ages, so I was not disputing this theory. Even though I was a very tall English-speaking *gussaq*, and she an extremely short speaker of Yup'ik Eskimo, we struck up a magical friendship.

Our friendship actually grew through my consideration of her stature. I tapped the children and young adolescents and motioned for them to sit down when they came and stood in front of us. She really liked that.

In both Aboriginal and Maori traditional ceremonies I knew that elders reprimanded children who acted disrespectfully. I thought of Paratai and what she would have done. So I didn't hesitate. I was very surprised that the children even stood there. It seemed they were totally unaware of these elders.

I had noticed that the elders were extremely shy. In the old days their authority would have been recognised and respected, and they would not have needed to discipline children in these circumstances. I knew my friend would not have been able to see anything with those standing in front, but I also knew she would have done nothing about it if I had let people stand in front of us. I motioned the kids in front several times and they seemed to be getting the idea. They were mesmerised by the dancing too.

After a while I noticed that my friend reached out a cragged little hand, and then a fur covered boot, and gave her own tap and small kick when she couldn't see. She then nudged me and giggled. I gave her the thumbs up sign. She enjoyed it. So did I. Other elders along the line nodded and smiled approvingly at me.

In front of us we had the best-behaved children in the room. As they came in the children immediately plunged to the floor and checked back that we could see. Everyone was happy. My friend looked a bit disappointed when I left, but I knew she could keep up the good work we'd achieved together. I wondered if I had started a mutiny of elders sweeping along the Yukon River, reclaiming their rights.

I could hear Paratai's voice in my head, 'That's right, darling.' I knew she would be proud of me.

Chapter 32

Kotzman Returns

Kotzman landed once again at Christchurch airport. This time he took a cab to my parent's home where he spent the night. They dropped him at the train station in the morning so that he could catch the Southerner down to Balclutha. His only luggage was a suitcase and backpack. Everything else had been sold, stored at Beth's or mailed to me in Balclutha.

He was excited about the train journey. His father had worked for the railways all his life. Kotz had loved helping him. 'The smell of the railway is in my blood,' he reckoned.

My mother, who had been a home hairdresser, had given Kotzman a haircut and packed him a lunch for the journey by train. Six ham sandwiches, a large piece of homemade bacon and egg pie or 'bacon and egg cake', as Kotz called it, some fruit and a bottle of beer.

As he got closer, I got more and more excited. It seemed people were calling me from every place he had just been. I wanted him to finally get to me. We had agreed on a plan. We didn't want to draw undue attention to him turning up in the small town of Balcutha, so together we decided to smuggle him in. If he had some time to settle in without any social pressure, I could then take the time to introduce him properly. This way I would keep local gossip at bay. The excitement of this plan reminded me of an Enid Blyton 'Famous Five' adventure. In keeping with that I would need lemonade and cake for him on his arrival.

He would walk from the station, and back along the track. Then he would climb over the fence at the end of my road. I hung a rag on the fence on the rail side so he would know where to climb. He would then come down the short street and home through the back door. No one would ever see him. We both loved the idea of this covert approach, this stealth. My mountain man would come right back to my very own teacher flat, and nobody would know.

Kotzman knocked on my door late afternoon. It was just as we had planned. It was so wonderful to see him. He hugged me in a bone-crushing hug. Bel took one look at him and decided that from now on she was his and they were inseparable again. He decided to take her with him out to Kotahitanga that night.

He talked about the train journey for a long time afterwards. The meal my mother had packed for him was a hit. 'It was just right,' he told me over the afternoon tea I had made for us. 'Oh, and I loved the pretty yellow flowers growing alongside the railway lines.'

'Don't say that to any of the local farmers. That's gorse, a noxious weed.' I laughed. 'It drives the farmers nuts trying to get rid of it.'

'Well, they were still pretty,' he said. 'Just an amazingly great train ride.'

Later that evening we pulled up at his final destination, Kotahitanga. We could finally relax. His journey back to me was completed. It was August the eighth, 2000.

At Kotahitanga, Kotzman settled down to work on his educational paper. He was also keen to start pottering around tidying up the place. It was still cold. He had the little potbelly fire going all day and all night. 'Wow, it sure is cold out here,' he said when I visited him the next day. 'Reckon it could be colder than at Elmer's place.' I knew the wind blew straight off the sea and whistled through the walls. No central heating out here.

Kotzman quickly settled into a routine. He would rake up the fire and take Bel out along the beach. Then he would come back for coffee and some project or other he was working on. In the afternoon, when the sun shone through the windows into the lounge, he would plan his meals and do some reading. He invited me over for dinner regularly. He turned out to be quite a good cook.

I loved driving out on that country road to the sound of the rolling waves. I would smell fresh lamb chops and minted peas as I walked in the door. He knew I loved that dish. He was definitely trying to impress me.

We would walk for miles along the beach, talking and sharing our days. In the weekends I stayed out there with him. We worked on planting the garden with roses, and making Kotahitanga cosy and inviting.

I was busy in Balclutha with my schoolwork as well. With study and the choir I had joined, life was busy. It was such a contrast to have Kotahitanga and Kotzman to unwind with in the weekends. I was enjoying introducing him over dinners to my closest friends.

'Have you got a man out there?' some of my colleagues asked.

'Yeah, a mountain man from Alaska.'

'*Really?*' I smiled. Really.

I had taken Kotzman's trunks and boxes out to Kotahitanga and he was enjoying unpacking his special possessions. He always had something new to show me. Alaskan rugs, a wolf pelt, ivory carvings, even a mammoth tusk. It was so exciting to be able to see and touch these artefacts. I loved hearing the stories that came with each piece.

He then bought a truck, and I taught him to drive on the other side of the road. He had his international driver's licence, but it was several weeks before he felt confident enough to drive all the way into Balcutha.

'Remember,' I told him over and again, 'keep the steering wheel on the centre line.' That way I hoped he would remember to drive on the correct side of the road. There had been many accidents caused by tourists forgetting this essential rule out in the country.

Every time he got into the car, little Bel would climb up in the front passenger seat. That was something I had never allowed her to do. She would turn and check that I could see her. Then she would peer over the top of the windscreen with importance as they drove off, travelling the roads together.

Kotzman also bought a small dinghy to row in the stream that ran at the bottom of our hill. He spent his days fly-tying and honing his cooking skills. Paddling and cooking, writing and reading and walking.

The lawn mowing and garden also kept him busy, and he tried to get into the brand new habit of stopping for morning tea. I left him baking during the week. He loved this new schedule of stopping mid morning and afternoon for a 'refuel,' as he put it.

Kotzman painted, cleaned, mended and practised hard to impress me in the kitchen. I was very impressed all round. We were in love.

Chapter 33

Winter Activities in Alaska

It was now midwinter at Pilot Station, and with it never-ending winter sports activities. Compared with the more mellow and relaxed feel of autumn, winter in bush Alaska was hectic and exhausting. The days were shorter. Sun was up by 10 am and gone again by 1:30 pm. Temperatures hovered between minus 40 and minus 10 degrees Celsius. One day our thermometer reached minus 50 degrees. As far as I was concerned any temperature under minus ten was just freezing. Although some days at minus 20 degrees with the sun out it seemed not too cold at all.

I had begun the long and tedious task of becoming certified to teach in the United States. The more essential application for residency had ground to an apparent standstill. Week after week I called, waiting for any word of my application processing from the US Immigration Department in Southern California. It had begun to take on a fantasy aspect, somehow coupled in my mind with Disneyland. Maybe both organisations lived in the same dream world.

As luck would have it, five months after 9/11 the US Department of Homeland Security had decided to reinvent a more thorough system of checking for all residency applications. Given the amount of interest I had already spawned in Homeland Security at LA airport, my residency application did not bear thinking about. I pushed it to the back of my mind and concentrated on the necessary exams at hand. Passing these exams would certify me as a competent teacher of the brand new national standards of the No Child Left Behind policy. President George W Bush had signed this act into law almost on the day that I landed back in Alaska.

The Praxis exams were to be held in the high school mid March. The dreaded Praxis exam, mandatory for all teachers to become certified under the No Child Left Behind (NCLB) Act, was an American based wide ranging test of 'simple' mathematics, American grammar, reading and writing. I needed to start studying.

Specialist teachers had been ordered to pass a further Praxis exam in their specialised subject area. One of the problems for teachers out in the bush was that owing to the small size of classes, many teachers had to teach a variety of subjects in order to cover the curriculum. No specialist teacher could be hired simply for the luxury of specialising in one subject. This meant that the middle and high school teachers now needed to be tested in depth in each of the multiple subject areas they taught. This translated to huge amounts of study and stress. It also presented the possibility that if a teacher should fail a test, that subject would then become unavailable as part of the school's curriculum. As principal responsible for all student education, this situation had Gary grinding his teeth most nights.

Loud drones of bush planes delivering and sending student teams of basketball players on interschool weekend matches became the symphony of late Friday afternoons, Saturdays and Sundays. The students slept on the classroom floors. This meant much more work for the faculty and cooks, clearing classrooms and organising volunteers. People were needed to man the scoreboard, referee, manage student groups, and cook up breakfasts, lunches and dinners, as well as organise post-match dances. The techno-pumping discotheques with pounding bass and counterpoint of screaming snow machines reverberated deep into the nights. They were all designed to impress anyone and everyone.

Even though the law stated, 'No snow machines after 10pm', there was no VPO (Village Police Officer) willing to enforce that law in Pilot Station. So this fell into the realm of 'other duties' that were part of a principal's yearly contract. Gary's disappearing coat tails and telephone voice seemed to be the only physical reminders of him in weekends.

One day when Gary came home for lunch, he brought me a treat from the social studies class. They had been making *akutaq*.

'Eskimo ice cream, honey,' Gary explained. He was carrying a small bowl with a mixture that looked a like a blob of cake mix with berries scattered through it.

'Wow! Joy Cowley wrote to me about this.' I had received another letter from her the week before.

'Don't worry,' he laughed, 'it's not the real stuff. It is what some of the younger ones make now with what they can buy from the store.'

'Oh?' It would contain more sugar, presumably. I took a small spoonful. All I could taste were berries.

'Yeah they use Crisco, rather than deer tallow. Easier to get.' Crisco was a vegetable shortening so I was pleased I had taken only a small teaspoonful. Although I knew I would get to taste the real stuff one day, I wasn't in any rush. I was still plucking up courage to attempt to cook the large side of moose meat in our freezer.

Tim, our neighbour, bought a dozen extra large pizzas back from Anchorage as a treat for the kids' weekend academic decathlon. As he had no room to store the pizzas in his freezer, he had simply left them on our mutual back doorstep for a week.

'Tim,' I announced one evening when I had been over watching *The Godfather* on their DVD player. 'I saw fox tracks near the pizza boxes on the back door step.'

'Yeah, I saw those too.'

'Well, wouldn't it be a shame if the foxes ate them before the kids had a chance?'

'Emma, they can't smell frozen food.' Oh, how silly. I blushed. I sometimes forgot we were living in a vast natural freezer.

Often during the weekend games the weather would close in, and the teams would be stuck at the school longer than the weekend. Flights were abandoned one after another. Consequently the principal and teachers spent most of the weekend supervising students in the school gym.

Almost all the staff seemed to spend their entire weekends at the school. This was different from the schools in New Zealand. In Alaska teachers were paid an extra allowance for extra duty activities. School coaches were paid, hired and fired. Coaching contracts were keenly sought after as extended income.

Gary looked pleased when he turned up for lunch one day.

'We've got extra funding mid February to start after-school programmes,' he said, smiling proudly.

I pushed my study papers away. Any excuse.

'After-school programmes like what?' I asked. The mind boggled.

'Homework classes. Teachers'll be paid about 25 bucks a session. They *will* be pleased.' Taking a couple of kids after school each day for 'catch up,' would add a lot of extra income to a teacher's pay packet over a week. It would also mean better opportunities for our school students to pass the state exams.

There was a lot of flu around. Staff seemed particularly prone. I made it my responsibility to deliver flasks of boiled ginger water à la Paratai, chicken soup and Vicks Vapour Rub, and lend a sympathetic ear. They were all very grateful. I felt like camp mother.

'You know, Emma,' Susan told me after I had dropped off more ginger water to her for her cough. 'It feels a bit like entering a cess pool in the elementary school at the moment.' I nodded sympathetically.

I could well imagine that. 'I just can't wait for the opening of the new school.'

One evening about 6 pm we were startled to hear a very loud helicopter overhead. I had asked a junior class once did they know what a helicopter was. Experiences out here were very limited. 'Do any of you know what a bus, train, wheelbarrow, beach and garden are?' Nope, but they all knew about helicopters.

The helicopter was an army Iroquois. The noise was so deafening I was sure it was either going to land on top of our house or right next to us, but it deferred to the airstrip. In the following three minutes I counted 24 snow machines and one pickup truck headed up to the airstrip.

A Year 10 student had gone into premature labour during a maths lesson that morning. The teacher's aide had gone to Gary.

'Help. Lisa is having her baby! Her waters have broken!'

'Don't panic, I'll take her to the medical centre,' he had calmly responded. Oh, the joys of being a principal in the bush.

It eventuated that the workers at the medical centre decided to call in the helicopter because the baby was one month premature. A helicopter was needed to take the mother to Bethel in a prone position. It was almost impossible to fly prone in a bush plane, some local mothers had told me. In Bethel the contractions were stopped and the girl returned to school.

Teenage pregnancy was normal here. It was expected by families and celebrated. Often a baby would be expected at graduation time. There was little motivation to pursue further education, and yet the talent to do so was so often present. It had the teachers gnashing their teeth with frustration at the great educational losses they perceived.

Chapter 34

A Proposal

On the day I turned 50 Kotzman proposed to me. We had left Balclutha as soon as school was out and were staying at my parents' home in Christchurch, having arrived the night before. My father and Kotz had gone for a beer at the local working-man's club when we arrived in Christchurch. I found out later it was Kotz's opportunity to ask my father's permission for my hand.

'Are you capable of keeping my daughter in the lifestyle to which she wants to become accustomed?' My father deadpanned. Once Kotz caught the twinkle of merriment in his eyes he relaxed. They had laughed and toasted together.

Kotzman brought a breakfast tray to my bedroom the following morning. There was a cup of hot tea, and thinly sliced toast specially prepared and cut the way my father did each day for my mother, with raspberry jam and Vegemite. Kotz and my father had both been in the kitchen, talking and preparing trays for their women.

Kotzman stood holding the tray. He began to warble the birthday song, smiling proudly with his proffered treat. 'Happy birthday to you. Happy birthday to you. Happy birthday, dear Sunshine. Happy birthday to you.'

He placed the tray on my bed. A vase with a pink camellia from the garden sat in one corner. A small woven basket with a lid was on the other.

'What's that?' I asked. 'A present!'

He grinned. 'Open it.'

The basket was about ten centimetres tall with a fitted lid. The weaving was black and white and fine. On the very top of the lid there was a delicately carved walrus head with tiny black eyes and tusks made of ivory. It was beautiful, delicate.

'It's made of baleen. In the old days the Inupiaq men wove these baskets as special gifts,' he explained.

'Oh wow, I love it! ' I exclaimed.

'Lift the lid,' he urged me. I lifted the lid. Inside was a green velvet box. Kotz moved over to the side of the bed and knelt down. As I lifted out the box he asked, 'Sunshine, will you marry me?'

'Of course, sweetheart!' I opened the box. The ring was beautiful. Eight diamonds surrounded a central heirloom diamond. He kissed me.

'It represents the eighth of August,' he explained. That was the day he had come back to me in New Zealand.

That evening we went back to the working-men's club. Kotz had told me he loved to dance, and there was a band playing that night. My parents both came with us for a celebratory meal and drink.

Once the band started my parents were up on the dance floor. It didn't take long for Kotzman to ask me to dance. Kotz had asked the band to play the Tennessee Waltz. Apparently it had been his father's favourite song. He whirled me around so much I was dizzy. Others sat down to watch. We had a ball. I so enjoyed moving in his arms to the music.

'He sure can dance,' said my father as we sat down. He and my mother were holding hands and smiling happily at us. They left shortly after.

'Sunshine, remember, you will never have to leave home again. I love you. I love New Zealand like you do. It is home for me too.'

We danced and danced and danced.

Chapter 35

A Sunday Afternoon Ride

The school truck was now replete with chains and Gary would constantly pick up students from neighbouring villages as they arrived to compete and camp out for the weekend in the school gym. At minus 30 degrees now most days, it was far too cold for anyone to be left for any time outside. With changeable and freezing weather, there were constant random call-outs.

I had received from the English teacher a very large package of past test-sheets in Praxis general subjects, to practice on. My confidence had been severely shaken when I kept getting many of the test items wrong. Up till then I had been thinking I could easily pass basic reading, writing and maths tests, but now the truth lay before me. I couldn't.

I tried blaming it on Americanisms but I had to admit that the maths sheets contained few of these. I struggled on with my study, my self-esteem withering at every page.

I knew it was theoretically possible to keep sitting these tests until one passed, but apart from funding the $100 test fee, sitting the Praxis test while living in bush Alaska posed added problems. First there were the unpredictable delays in ordering and receiving the papers at our outpost. Next there was the job of finding someone qualified and prepared to be the official test supervisor. This had to be a professional educator with no personal conflict of interest. That was a very difficult person to find when other faculty members were also sitting. Many were partners of the teachers sitting the tests, so they could not qualify. Then there remained the almost insurmountable challenge of gathering supervisor and test sitters together in an uninterrupted block of time.

With the activities schedule in full 24-hour swing it seemed to me that the only available time would be between 1 am and 4 am on a Sunday morning. However, I did gain comfort knowing I was not about to sit alone. All the teachers had to sit and pass these tests now in order to be deemed highly qualified as part of the NCLB Act. As well, everyone wanted the credentials before the next round of teacher contracts due in April.

My strident complaints were only a small mutter in the general cacophony of teacher anguish. In order to prepare everyone for my dismal failure well ahead of time, I constantly reminded anyone who was interested that I was the only non-American and my completely 'different' educational background gave me a huge disadvantage.

Gary had bought us a snow machine. A two-up. He had paid one of the men in the village to ride it back for us from St Mary's. We decided to take it out the first opportunity the very next weekend. A Sunday afternoon jaunt. Although Gary had ridden snow machines extensively before, it was my first time.

We both needed a snow machine trip out as a welcome respite from stress.

Gary was excited to be out riding a snow machine again. The sun was out and I spent a good half hour of it dressing for the ride; Gary had drilled me in the importance of wearing the correct clothing in these freezing conditions. This time my heavy-duty gear also included goggles and three pairs of gloves. I grabbed the camera, not wanting to miss the opportunity to take some shots of this landscape for others to enjoy. I waddled down the steps to the waiting machine.

The machine was like a low-slung motorbike with skis on the front and a large track that was driven off the motor at the back. We needed no roads; the machine was designed for snow and ice and apparently at high speeds could even negotiate water. I had ridden many a motorbike in my teenage years, but this seemed much less safe. I hadn't realised just how close to the ground we were going to be. It was also much more noisy and smelly than I was used to. With both of us on board we took off at a rather sedate pace.

On our first turn over the snow bank we were both thrown into the snow. Gary apologised, 'Sorry, honey, have to get used to the added weight behind.' He was finding there was much more limited manoeuvrability with two aboard.

'It's okay.' I dusted myself off. That hadn't been as bad as I thought. Landing in the snow was a soft and pleasant surprise. I felt much more confident as I climbed back on.

In ten minutes we were up at the airstrip and heading out on the tundra beyond. We had looked for berries in October out here. It was now pristine white. I wanted to get a photo. Prolonged thudding on Gary's heavy jacket eventually elicited a response, and we stopped.

I dismounted, removing my goggles and top gloves, and my right top mitten. I still had on thermal gloves. Within 30 seconds, my face exposed to the weather felt like a plate glass window. My finger touching the cold of the camera, even through my thermal glove, began to seriously freeze. However, as a *cheechako*, a newcomer to Alaska, I ignored these signs. I concentrated instead on pointing the camera in the best possible direction for a landscape photo.

I didn't want to complain, as we had been out so rarely. I wanted to enjoy this special time together on this beautiful if rapidly dimming day. Gary turned to me.

'Wanna try driving this?' he asked. My finger was throbbing. Reluctantly I arranged my frozen face into what I hoped was an interested expression. Gary had already told me he wanted to make sure I knew how to manage the machine in case of any emergency.

He showed me how it worked. I was surprised to discover that the accelerator was a thumb button on the right hand. 'Just squeeze it to go faster, no gears.' That was all very straightforward.

'How do I stop?'

'Well, there is a brake on the left handlebar, but all everyone else does is remove their thumb from the throttle. With no acceleration the machine will stop.' I wondered why I had felt reluctant to try to drive the confounded thing. It seemed so easy. This petrol-smelling lawn mower that sounded like it was stuck in first gear doing 100 kilometres an hour might actually be fun after all.

Putting my mitten and glove back on over my now constantly throbbing finger, I pulled down my goggles. Gary got off, and I sat up the front. I would have a go on my own. His last words echoed in my head as I roared off at one mile per hour. 'Always turn in a wide arc so as not to tip!'

Well, that piece of information came in handy immediately. To my great consternation my right hand was now aching terribly with the cold. I found the throttle very hard to manage. I was also discovering that the machine was starting to act like a horse I once had. When I took the reins it just went wherever it wanted. Compared to flying a plane where a touch of the joystick can tip the wings at alarming angles, the snow machine steering seemed to lie at the other end of the continuum. In fact I was thinking a monkey wrench would be an extremely useful tool to have. I needed one to drag the steering at least one-degree off straight ahead.

My snow machine and I were travelling away at ponderous speed further and further from Gary. We were inscribing the largest arc ever on the face of this snow plateau on the Lower Yukon. We were leaving knowledge, love, survival skills and sympathy way behind.

I imagined Gary calling out to me. 'Look out for the bears, trees, frozen sheets of ice hiding enormous chasms from which there is no escape!' Or, 'Where are you heading, you silly woman?' Anyway there was no way I could hear him. The snow machine screamed in power-filled and headstrong delight. The resonance of the motor was shaking snow from the topmost branches in the valleys for miles around.

At a point when I thought I must disappear over the brink of the distant hill ahead, never to be seen again, I noticed that I was actually vaguely turning. Over my left shoulder I could see Gary standing way in the distance. He wasn't jumping up and down in agitation. Maybe all was well. Gaining my first modicum of bravery, I attempted to lean out on the machine and pull the handlebars to the left as I had seen others do. Rather like a motorbike heading into a stiff curve. That did not work. The machine ploughed on dead ahead.

I noticed that the pine trees on the distant ridge were definitely looming. I was also making them move now gradually along my right side. The machine and I were rounding and actually making our way back. Somewhere in that square mile Gary was standing.

I saw him in the distance at the point where my arms were quivering in strain. I was pulling so hard on the handlebars to make this curve, I couldn't manage the effort any longer. I eventually pulled up quite some distance from him. He trekked his way across the snow to where the quieted machine and I now sat.

'How was that?' He was sweating in the exertion of the long trek to my side.

'Fine.' I smiled cheerfully back. I was safe. No way would I ever drive one of these things again. 'It's a bit hard to turn, though.'

'Yes, honey. You'd have found it much easier if you had picked up a little speed.' He patted my shoulder in support. I whipped out my camera to take a pretend shot of my final resting place. I needed time to absorb that piece of useful information. However the camera was frozen solid. As well, my right hand was now in absolute agony.

'Please,' I asked, 'could you unzip my parka so I can stuff my hand in to warm it up?' He unzipped my parka and I thrust my frozen hand under my left armpit.

'Are you okay, honey?' he asked.

'Yep,' I lied.

'Where would you like to go?'

'Let's head for that ridge around the top of the village.' I climbed back on behind him. The weather looked as if it was beginning to close in, and I wanted to see the village from another perspective. I wasn't too sure I'd ever want to come out riding like this again.

As we rode along much faster now, I tried to sit on my hand and keep my parka close to my ears as the wind snatched and tore at my skin. It was so icy. After a while the pain in my hand became so bad it felt like it had frozen solid. I tapped Gary and we headed for home.

'Go for a ride on your own!' I yelled as we pulled up. I knew he was longing to do a proper ride. He headed joyfully off, the throttle finally opened wide. I took the steps up to the house two at a time.

Entering our warm house I frantically searched for some woollen gloves. I ripped off my outer clothes and paced around. I never wanted to stop for one moment. I wanted the moving to distract myself from the agonising pain.

I eventually found the gloves. I continued moving around the house. I was constantly shaking my right-gloved hand over and over to get the blood circulation going. Eventually the pain started to subside. As it gradually diminished I could finally focus on making a hot cup of tea.

Gary returned, elated at his fast ride. He was immediately alerted to a problem as he saw my clothes scattered all over the floor. I was sitting nursing a hot mug of tea.

'Your hand?' he asked, searching my face for clues.

'Yep, it got a bit frozen.'

'Why didn't you tell me?' He looked displeased. 'We could easily have come straight back.'

'I didn't want to ruin our first run,' I said lamely. Tears were welling up in my eyes. It had all been very painful. Gary was extremely concerned about the extent of the discomfort that I had hidden from him while we were out. He gave me a cuddle.

'The bush is no place for bravado, especially in winter,' he admonished gently. 'It is far too easy to get frostbite.' I nodded. I could see that. I was learning fast the dangers of even a simple Sunday jaunt in bush Alaska.

Chapter 36

Spring Planning

Following our engagement we had decided to take Paratai's advice. 'No point waiting when you are older, darling. May as well just do it straight away.' We set the date for January 2001, during my summer school holidays.

I was very reluctant to continue with my studies. The resource teacher training had just finished, and our group was celebrating the end of all that study. I was now a fully qualified New Zealand Resource Teacher of Learning and Behaviour.

'Only one more year, sweetheart,' Gary urged me. 'Then you'll have finally completed your masters degree.'

Over the past few months Kotzman, my Alaska wild man, had completely metamorphosed into Gary. Gary, my American fiancé.

Deep down I knew he was making sense. It was something I had dreamed of. I could credit the studies I had just finished towards my masters degree. I had three more papers to write over one year. Then it would be done.

The wedding was a much more pleasant distraction from the thoughts of another year of self-discipline and essay writing. I called Ella one school night and asked her to be my bridesmaid. She loved the idea.

'I've asked Jenny to be the maid of honour,' I added.

'Fantastic!' Ella and Jenny enjoyed each other's company. 'What are we wearing?' Ella asked me.

'It'll be very low key, darling. I told Jenny just to wear anything she liked. I'm going to wear that long green dress. The one you talked me into buying in Sydney.'

'Yeah?' She sounded a bit surprised. 'That green and gold dress you got in Balmain?'

'Yes. So wear anything that you would like to wear, sweetheart.'

'Okay.' She sounded disappointed. She had recently featured on the cover of a bridal magazine in Sydney, as part of her in-house modelling job. The bridal outfit she wore was a full skirt in orange silk and a white silk blouse. There had been huge billboards with her photo on them around the city. I guessed my long green dress was a bit tame after that.

Unbeknown to me, Ella rang Jenny. They plotted colour-coordinated outfits together. Friday night Ella was back on the phone.

'Mum, about the wedding,' she started. Hmm, had she changed her mind about being bridesmaid? 'I've spoken with Jenny and she agrees with me. We want to wear something to match your dress.'

'What?' Both together were a bit formidable.

'Well, we can each afford to have a dress made to match yours.'

'You really want to do that?' I was surprised. I was trying to imagine them plotting this on the phone together.

'Yeah, we do. Is that okay with you?'

'Well actually . . .' I thought for a moment. My stomach turned with excitement. 'Actually I would *love* that. What colour did you two come up with?'

'Jenny wants to talk to you about it.'

I rang Jenny immediately. She sounded a bit embarrassed.

'Look, if you don't mind. Um, Ella and I had a chat about it.' She sounded apologetic. 'We both would really like to do something a bit more special for you than simply wear one of our own dresses.'

'Well, that's all *I'll* be doing,' I reminded her. 'I don't want you to go to any trouble or expense.' It wasn't as if I were a young thing getting married for the first time.

'Yes, but we want to match you. We thought maybe a dark forest green?' I thought about my gold and dark green dress.

'Oh wow, Jenny, that'd be lovely! I'd really *love* it.' I felt a surge of bridal excitement. Jenny had been quite a seamstress when we were in school. Her taste was impeccable, and she paid attention to the smallest details. I totally trusted whatever she came up with. We made a girls' date for me to go to Christchurch, stay with Jenny and have a look for material.

Ella, of course, was a house model. As a standard size ten, she was modelling the in-house fashion designs for buyers. She would be stunning in anything. This wedding was going to be pretty amazing. All matching. I went straight to my wardrobe and pulled out the long, patterned, green dress. I tried it on.

I loved the way the long sleeves flared at the wrists. I liked the fitted bodice and the slight flare of the skirt, the lower neckline with its lace-up, and the subtle gold shot through it. Hmm, I'm not sure it is going to be enough though, I mused. Especially with Jenny and Ella in matching outfits. I studied myself again in the mirror. I had to stand on the bed to get the effect of the full length. Maybe a soft sheer long coat made to go over the top would look good, I wondered. I tried to turn and look at myself from behind. I grabbed the net curtain away from the window and draped what I could over the dress. I could picture a small train. Maybe a soft coat worn over the dress with a small train? Maybe an effect like that in gold would look bridal. I was getting more and more excited.

'Ella rang,' I told Gary when I went out to Kotahitanga that night. 'Apparently this wedding is going to be all colour coordinated. Jenny and Ella want to wear dark forest green. Just like the colour of the New Zealand bush.'

'Great,' Gary stood and gave me a big hug. 'I'll get a dark green shirt to go with my suit.' Gary had decided he wanted a good dark suit. A New Zealand wool suit.

We travelled up to Christchurch during the long weekend of the Canterbury Show in mid November. We had some shopping to do.

Gary spent the first night with my parents, while Jenny and I plotted and planned at her place. Gary wanted to work with Honey, teaching her to walk on her leash without pulling, so he said he would come over the following day.

On Saturday Jenny and I went shopping. I'd told her about my idea for a long gold coat. I'd since seen some gold curtain material in Balclutha that looked like it might be perfect. I'd brought along a snippet. Jenny hesitated. '*Curtain* material? Well, let's look,' she said.

The first material shop we visited had exactly what we'd been looking for. Plain, dark-green, shiny material. It was the end of the roll. Enough for one long dress for Jenny and one short one for Ella. Perfect.

There was nothing quite as gold as my sample in the curtain material section in the shop, but with a longer net sample Jenny could now picture it. 'I think if we get some plain gold binding for the edges,' she mused, 'it could look great.' We then bought a couple of patterns.

After one hour we emerged with a couple of bags of goodies. We had everything we needed. The total price had been close to $150. The zips and binding had actually cost more than the material. We were pleased with ourselves. We headed for some coffee. Picking men's shirts in dark-green would be next.

We were home early afternoon, with the men's shirts. We had also found a great matching tie to show Gary.

My cousin Robert had been pleased to be Gary's best man. The men had had an immediate rapport when Robert and his wife had visited us in Balclutha. Robert and his wife worked in Wellington. They had been on a holiday travelling around the South Island, and had decided to call in and catch up with 'that Alaskan' and me.

Gary had news. 'Your dad,' he said when he arrived late afternoon, 'wonders what the shirts are like. He seems to be expecting to be in the wedding party.'

'Goodness me!' I was shocked. 'I never thought for a moment Dad would want to try to give me away again.' I seemed to keep coming back!

Gary and I drove back to Balclutha with our purchases – our material, shirts and ties. We'd left a matching shirt and tie for Dad. Gary had bought a brand new dark suit. He looked quite handsome in it.

We'd also bought some dark-green card to make invitations, along with a gold stamp featuring a koru – a traditional New Zealand symbol based on the whorl of an unopened fern frond. Jenny had been brilliant in finding all these supplies. All I needed now was to organise flowers and cake. That would be easy. Roses abounded in Balclutha, and the little local cake shop was excellent. That would do fine.

I had arranged for a local dressmaker in Balclutha to make the bridesmaids' dresses. She came widely recommended from everyone, and I could not believe how inexpensive it would be to have her sew for us. She said all she needed was the measurements, and the dresses would each only need one final fitting. That fitting could be scheduled for the day before. She told me how much material I would need for my long coat. It would be slippery sewing, but she thought she could do it.

Gary and I found a lovely little country church between Milton and Balclutha. It was set right in the middle of farmland. Sheep were grazing all around. It seemed fitting somehow. For the reception, there was a country bed and breakfast homestead available just up the road. Everything was falling into place.

Chapter 37
A Job Offer

In Alaska's freezing daily conditions, I needed to cover up well before heading out. I timed my excursions around midday, while it was light. I had discovered on one of my treks to the post office that the freezing air immediately made the inside of my nose freeze solid, my eyelashes too. I wanted to collect the local paper from the post office. With no daily newspaper deliveries out here, it was an important way to keep up with local news.

The Iditarod Trail Sled-Dog Race took place during January. This epic dog-team race was run from Anchorage to Nome. The 1000-kilometre trail took about two weeks to complete. Contestants came from all over Alaska and the world. Although the race was run far from Pilot Station, it was the news topic of the day. Students used the web to follow the husky teams' progress.

A local event, the Kuskokwim 300 was held before the Iditarod. The K300, as it was popularly known, started in Bethel and stretched between small villages along the Kuskokwim River. At half the length of the Iditarod, it gave world-class teams the opportunity to train for the big one.

The local Kuskokwim Delta newspaper, published monthly, arrived in our village sporadically. I read that the overflow on top of the river ice had made the trail difficult during the recent K300. The locals held those who could negotiate physical conditions like these in the highest esteem. In the end out here, in life in general, it was always a matter of humans versus the elements.

The K300 spawned local races. With weather and snow conditions excellent for sledding, one weekend in March our village hosted our own local 'dog races'. These teams of huskies were not nearly as common as they once were. The noisy snow machine or sno-go had replaced dog team transport. In this changed subsistence economy, providing enough food for hungry dog teams was a chore few chose. Most preferred purchasing petrol to run a sno-go. Elders were not impressed with this replacement. 'Sno-go not come home in whiteout,' they said. 'Not eat sno-go if stranded and hungry.'

Gary was home for lunch with some momentous news. 'Honey,' he said, giving me a bear hug, 'I'm sorry, but there won't be any teaching positions here next year for you.' I sat down in shock. 'No one wants to move.'

For the first time in memory this year no staff wanted to move on. Everyone was keen to move into the brand new school buildings. 'You know, with the new faculty housing as well,' he continued gently, 'it is an incentive for everyone to stay.'

'Okay,' I breathed out hard. That was a huge shock. 'What do we do now?'

'There's possibly room for you in another school in the district.' Gary looked serious. He had just had a phone call from the elusive superintendent.

'What do you think about that?' I asked him. I was trying to gauge what he was thinking. If I had to move to another school area, weather and work would dictate any opportunities we might have to be together. Also, if we had to live in separate houses we would be unable to save the same as we could by living together.

'Absolutely not on. Having come this far to be together, there's no way I want you living in a neighbouring village. Just not an option, is it.'

I breathed out in relief. I didn't like that idea either.

'No, I don't think so either.'

'It's okay, honey, we'll both just look elsewhere.'

Although it would mean packing again, I found the prospect of moving to a new village together rather exciting.

In bush Alaska the quality of life in the village, along with the friendliness of the people, were serious considerations. Word travelled swiftly around these remote places, stimulated by the relatively small populations of itinerant teachers. Some villages were known to be hostile and difficult to work in. In some places family pets would go missing and teachers were objects of ongoing harassment. In areas where alcoholism and vandalism ran together, maintaining teachers throughout the school year, even when they were on a signed contract, was extremely difficult.

Villages where there was local initiative, where councils followed rules, and where elders were honoured were much more rare. However, these villages that welcomed and appreciated teachers were more difficult to find. But teaching couples had an advantage. They tended to settle for longer periods of time, and were generally easier to accommodate and more reliable.

As well, each school district negotiated its own pay schedule, and they varied dramatically. The schools most difficult to access often had the highest pay rates. The most popular and closest to civilisation had the lowest. We needed to save. It was March, and the search was on. I badly needed to pass the Praxis exams.

Each week the increase in daylight hours seemed quite marked. Around this time a houseguest made a memorable comment during his stay. The internal house temperature had plunged overnight as the furnace had gone out. We discovered in the morning that this was because we had had a heavy blizzard overnight that nearly buried the entire village.

Asked if he had felt the cold, our guest's understated reply made me chuckle for a few days. 'Yes,' he said, 'I noticed it was a bit nippy.' At minus ten degrees inside, nippy it was indeed.

Gary guffawed at my own comment a couple of days later, when I said, 'Gee, it's warm today, I'll check the temperature. Oh yeah, it's zero degrees.' Anyone would've thought I had told the greatest joke of all time.

'Did you hear what you just said, honey?' He snorted. I replayed my comment in my head to check for idiotic translations. All appeared fine.

'Yeah,' I said slowly, giving him a puzzled but hopefully still intelligent look. We were using an outdoor Fahrenheit thermometer that we could read from inside the window. It read 0 degrees.

'You said it must be warm because it's zero degrees!' He chortled in delight.

'Well it *is*. I just checked!' I frowned. 'What's so funny about that?'

'Can you imagine saying that last winter?' He continued to chuckle. I guess I could sort of see the amusing aspect. I giggled. It was funny how I had become acclimatised so quickly.

Gary had been contacted by another school district in the south west of Alaska. They had heard that he was looking for a job. It amazed me how word seemed to travel fast, even when we were so far out in the bush.

'I've only heard excellent things about this district,' Gary enthused. 'It's further south, so easier to fly into as well. They know about you and are keen.'

I was still no further along with my immigration. Once cleared by immigration, in order to go on a payroll, I would need to get a social security number. I also desperately needed to pass the Praxis.

'I'm going to need to get some academic credits for my certification,' I said to Gary. Papers in Alaskan Studies were mandatory for Alaskan certification. 'It will take another year to complete those.' I was worried. It would require a lot more work.

We agreed to a telephone interview for the new positions. The interview was held in Gary's office on a conference call line. After the few jokes about my accent the talk quickly became casual, focusing much more on the local hunting and fishing in the district, rather than the work.

'I'd love to take you out fly fishing,' the female interviewer said. 'The fishing is spectacular, probably like New Zealand. Heaps of men from the Lower 48 fly out here to do their Alaskan thing.'

Gary raised his eyebrows at me in excitement. It all sounded great.

'We'd love to have you two here,' was how the conference finished. It seemed that the district office were keen for us to come. We would need to travel to Anchorage for the Alaska Teacher Job Fair early April. There we would meet the superintendent of this school district and hopefully sign the contracts to work.

I knew the Job Fair was the place where all districts recruited their teachers. Each school district would set up a booth in the large hotel ballroom there. Advertising was aimed at drawing the best teachers. Offers of housing, health care, transport and lucrative contracts were given as incentives. It would be interesting to see education strutting its stuff.

After I had counted and photographed our meat supplies, I uncovered the disconcerting fact that we would need to eat one chicken a week until May to get through the backlog. Then there were numerous pork roasts, chuck steaks, smoked bacon packages, and other meat parcels carefully wrapped and labelled by the supplier.

The meat was excellent. I thought Kiwis would be very impressed. It had been farm killed rather than factory killed, and the difference in taste was obvious. I was relieved to discover when I examined the meat cache that those disconcerting dozen packets or so of 'corned beef' in fact read 'chicken breasts' once I'd put my glasses on. It would be much quicker to plough through those in the allotted time. I still had some moose meat and one very large turkey.

The faculty members were upset that they were going to lose Gary, and so were the elders. It was humbling for him to be so appreciated in such a short time. Everyone understood our reasons for leaving.

The school year was drawing to a close, and with it came the lengthening days of spring and thaw.

'Graduation coming up,' said Gary one breakfast. 'I have so many testing schedules to meet and paperwork to complete.' I knew this was a frantic time of the year winding up the school. As well, the entire school needed to be packed up along with the office, ready for the big move up the hill.

Chapter 38

Preparations for the Big Day

Haere mai

Emma and Gary
invite you to share their wedding at Lovells Flat Church, Milton
Sat Jan 20th 2001 at 4 pm. Reception at Garvan Homestead.

A week before our wedding, our guests began arriving. Some wanted the chance to visit and explore the beautiful South Otago countryside. They were travelling from Auckland, Wellington, Sydney and Christchurch. We booked motels in Milton and Balclutha. We also had room at Kotahitanga in the sleep out. Paratai would be staying out there with Gary.

My primary school teacher from Whanganui was flying in from Auckland. My beloved teacher, who had inspired my own career, had kept in touch with me throughout all these years. She would be staying with my parents in a motel in Milton.

Jenny arrived in Balclutha laden with goodies. She was staying with me in the spare room of my little teacher flat.

'I've brought us some food,' she smiled. 'So we won't need to worry about cooking.' She'd brought vegetarian dishes, casseroles and all sorts of baking. Typically thoughtful, I thought. What a good friend she was.

Ella flew in from Sydney with Jane, her girlfriend. Merv and Evelyn offered them their spare room. They could sleep next door.

I had ordered bouquets of roses from a local Balclutha florist. The Leonidis roses were in perfect condition in late January. My own bouquet had been copied from my parents' 1946 wedding bouquet. Green ferns tumbled through the brick-red roses, giving the bouquet a true New Zealand feel.

The chocolate sponge cake I had ordered for our wedding cake was large and square. It was to be filled with fresh whipped cream. The plain chocolate icing on the top was a platform for two small plastic computers I had found in a toy-shop. I cut out and wrote a special message for each screen. A small posy of roses and green fern sat on the top between the computers. A gold ribbon encircled the cake.

We had dress fittings at the local dressmakers for Ella and Jenny. Jenny's dress was in the same style as mine, long and fitted with long sleeves. Ella's was knee length and had short sleeves.

'Hey Mum, put yours on now,' Ella urged after the fittings were completed. I pulled out my dress, and went and put it on. The dressmaker helped me into the long gold coat she had made.

'Looks very good,' she mused satisfactorily, smoothing it, before I went back in to show Ella and Jenny.

'Ohh,' Jenny gasped when I reappeared. 'Ohh.'

'Oh *great*, Mum,' breathed Ella. Jenny, Jane and Ella all loved the sheer gold coat I had first visualised standing on my bed holding the curtain. It followed the line of the dress, fastened by a small hook in the front. The hook was placed right where I would be holding my flowers. The small train followed gliding over the carpet as I walked. The coat had definitely lifted the dress to the realm of bridal gown now.

'You were right, Jen,' I said trying not to look too vain. 'That gold bias has set off the coat perfectly.' The dressmaker had done an excellent job. She was rightfully proud of her work. She insisted that the minimal fee was plenty. We were all so pleased we tipped her for all her skill and positive gentle manner.

Ella needed something to wrap around her shoulders. Balclutha winds were cold after Sydney's warm January weather. 'Jane and I are going to wander around Balclutha now and look for a small gold stole. It's a bit cold here, Mum.'

We all had gold shoes. Gary's job had been to spray paint all our shoes to match. I set them outside on the coal bin to dry in the sun. I was so thrilled with mine. They were very comfortable and had a small heel so that I was not too much taller than usual. The shoes had leather soles, just right for dancing. I had found them at the Salvation Army shop in Milton.

We flew Paratai over for the ceremony. She had made us a huge fruit wedding cake as a surprise present. She had also dyed her hair jet-black for the happy occasion. We hardly recognised her.

The choir had been practising relentlessly the last few weeks. No one had missed even one of these rehearsals. It wasn't often we had a chance to sing in public. The choir was stunning and haunting in their renditions of 'Amazing Grace', 'The Irish Blessing', and 'Pokarekare Ana', Gary's favourite. I had written an extra verse in Maori for this last song and coached the choir through the pronunciation. For the last few weeks we had been adding the wedding items to our repertoire during our regular practices. Even though I wouldn't be singing them with the choir, I still wanted to be singing, standing alongside Gary at the altar.

John, our choirmaster, was a gentle but firm leader. He knew his music and knew how to get the best out of us. He was also an accomplished organist. He would be accompanying the hymns during the service.

Merv had gone to great trouble to find the right tape recorder and microphones.

'I want a perfect recording of this service,' he said, rifling through his boxes of equipment in his storage shed. He was gathering up and checking out all of his microphones. 'The tapes are going to be sent to

America and Alaska, you know,' he added, as if this fact was unknown to me. We would be mailing off recordings of the ceremony to Gary's family, who could not make our wedding.

On the eve of the wedding Jenny, Ella, Jane and I all drove out to Kaka Point restaurant for my 'last supper' before marriage. We sat in the window at the small beachside restaurant and watched the spectacular sunset.

'How're you feeling?' Ella asked.

'Good,' I answered. 'Just a bit scared.' That warranted another bottle of bubbly.

'Here's to being a bit scared on the eve of your wedding,' toasted Jane. We laughed happily. We wondered what Gary was doing.

At that time, Gary was out on the beach at Kotahitanga with Bel. He was enjoying quiet time alone. Paratai had gone over the road to Mona's late afternoon. The Maori priest Lem and his wife had all gone up there for dinner. Lem and his wife had become friends during my monthly visits to the church in Dunedin. They had recently moved to Christchurch. They had travelled back especially for our wedding.

Gary had been invited to dinner too, but he wanted some time alone before his big day. Wandering the beach with Bel was perfect for him.

Mona, Paratai, Lem and his wife enjoyed their evening together. Lem had a copy of the service order and shared it with them all. They decided together they wanted to add in another hymn. Paratai told them that Gary had mentioned to her that 'How Great Thou Art' had been a favourite hymn of his mother's. They decided to do some photocopies and add that to the ceremony in honour of Gary's mother.

The morning dawned fine but very windy. Ella, Jenny and I had a hairdresser's appointment late morning. It was the third time I had ever been to a hairdresser. Ella had convinced me that a hairdresser was needed for such a special occasion. I wanted to wear a Maori bone comb in my hair. The hairdresser would style my hair as usual and place it firmly for me.

About 9 am there was a major power cut in Balclutha because of the wind. A tree had knocked over a power line. For two hours in the morning I fretted that my hair appointment would have to be abandoned, as there was no power. However five minutes before our appointment time the power came back on. I would be coiffed to perfection.

We drove out to the Homestead for our lunch and to get dressed for the wedding. First we had lunch in the restaurant. As we settled to eat, the waitress brought me a handwritten note.

'Please come to the kitchen urgently.' I wondered what problem there could be. When I reached the kitchen, standing in the middle of the table was a lime-green wedding cake. I burst out laughing. I thought it had been something much more serious.

The cooks looked sternly at me. This was no time for laughter.

'This cake was made by an important Maori elder,' the chef said. She spoke in reverential tones.

'Yes, Paratai.' I chuckled.

I had received an urgent call from Gary early that morning. Where could he get some green food colouring?

'What on earth do you want green food colouring for?' I asked him. I couldn't imagine why he would need green food colouring on his wedding day.

'Paratai.' Was all he could say.

I learned later while she had been staying out at Kotahitanga with

Gary, Paratai had been schooling him in Maori language. They had been spending their days out on the beach.

'She needs it for icing for a wedding cake she has made us as a wedding present.' There was no point in saying we already had a wedding cake. A simple chocolate cake with plastic computers on the top.

'You can get some food colouring at the store in Milton,' I told him. 'See you later!' That would be an unexpected drive for him on this busy day, but he'd handle it fine.

Now here it was. Paratai's large fruitcake covered in lime-green icing. Paratai had tried to match the colour scheme of the wedding party. 'I think I put too much green in, darling,' she explained later.

I told the staff to cover it with ferns and natives from the garden. They had been frightened to touch a 'sacred cake made by an important Maori elder'.

I laughed. 'Of course you can,' I said. 'Paratai won't mind at all.'

The cake would be wonderful to keep and have for the many visitors after the wedding was over.

My parents arrived on their way to the church. Jenny and Ella would travel in one car. Dad and I would follow.

As we travelled the country road to the church I squeezed Dad's hand.

'I know I am doing the right thing,' I said to him.

'Me too,' he replied, and smiled tenderly.

Chapter 39

Another St Mary's Trip

One Saturday morning at 7 am a small group of us trudged over to the high school and, for three hours, sat the dratted Praxis exam. James supervised. I tried to keep my anxiety at a reasonable level, but it was a tense and serious business. Finishing my tests in the allotted time, I slipped out of the room. Others stayed on to sit further tests. I trudged home to sit in a stupor in front of the TV, praying that I would not have to repeat those tests again in the next round. There was still no news from the US Immigration Department.

Gary convinced me to go out on the snow machine again. He wanted to do a run to St Mary's. Longer daylight hours meant snow was melting, and therefore time was now limited for snow machining.

The following Saturday, Gary was free from commitments. Even though we woke to blizzard conditions, things appeared to be clearing by lunchtime. I agreed that we should 'go for it'. I would be keeping my gloves on this time.

Gary called James. 'We're headin' off to St Mary's about two, aiming to be back between four thirty and five,' he said.

'Stick to the river track,' James responded. 'Well marked and flat.'

'Okay.'

'The first marker is there to let trail travellers know to turn right. That's where you head off the Yukon River and up over the riverbank,' continued James. 'It's a small, discreet track disappearing into the trees.'

We found the track easily. It was marked with tripods of hewn branches six foot tall, roped together at the top like tepee frameworks. Exactly at the point where I started to wonder if we had veered off the track, a tripodic shape would loom up out of the snow.

The journey was exciting. After we had been travelling about four miles along the frozen Yukon River, the first marker appeared dead ahead. I waved a gloved hand over Gary's shoulder. He nodded and we turned right off the river and into the trees.

As we headed deeper and deeper along the trail, we found ourselves often travelling along sloughs, tributaries of the Yukon River. They were like small icy highways, frozen solid and relatively smooth to travel on. I had read about these in articles about the K300. These sloughs would be roughly 20 or so metres across, lined with embankments of saplings. Sometimes the rows of saplings were placed across the river, manmade fences to warn of soft ice.

I had just finished *Tisha*, the true story of a nineteen-year-old teacher who lived in remote Alaska in the early 1920s. Her hair-raising adventures were mandatory reading for all new teachers to bush Alaska. Images from *Tisha* now hovered in my mind as conscious reminders of all the potential dangers this journey could present.

I had learnt that yellow or brown ice depicted soft, partially frozen surfaces that were to be avoided at all costs. My eyes were constantly alert for those colours on the ice we were zooming across.

I was also continually expecting to see bears. It was hard to believe that bears could be hibernating at present. I thought that they probably did in the old days of mushing teams, but no bear in his right mind could hibernate to the sound of snow machines. However I saw no wildlife apart from a red fox trotting across the river about a hundred metres further on.

After 30 minutes of travelling we started seeing tiny ribbons of fluorescent orange and pink tied to branches along the trail. These ribbons appeared rather like the bands used in the Southland bush to warn that possum traps were laid there. Periodically a tin of coke or pop would appear threaded through a branch. This litter was a comforting reminder that we were on the right track.

We eventually passed into a heavily wooded area where the track became only as wide as the skis on the sno-go. The tracks here were deeply grooved through regular use. The grooves left no option for steering. It was rather like being on automatic pilot.

We had seen two other snow machines returning to Pilot Station. I was relieved that they were out on the wide-open spaces. On these narrow grooved tracks, any meeting with a machine travelling in the opposite direction would necessitate reverse, not an easy feat on a sno-go.

We made it to St Mary's in just under an hour. We had covered sixteen miles. The last part of the track was pure washboard torture. The bumps were regular and steep, and I caught myself exhaling expletives. Luckily the deafening two-stroke engine drowned out my voice. I needed consciously to relax as we passed over the bone-shattering jolts. This was made difficult wearing a crash helmet. Like trying to relax while balancing a pumpkin on your head.

'We need to leave by four at the latest so that we'll be back within daylight hours,' Gary reminded me as we waddled into the store.

We didn't buy much, but browsing was fun. The snowsuit I was wearing was heavy duty. It was also about six sizes too large. Walking was difficult with the crotch hanging around my knees. Gary had insisted I wear it. If I was unlucky enough to fall into a frozen river, it was designed to keep me alive at least for a short time. The top half of the suit was of a brilliant orange material to enable easy spotting by rescuers.

We bought a few grocery items, including some diet coke. Although not a fan of pop, it would make a change from the cranberry juice and local distilled water supplies. We also bought a small bag of fresh baby potatoes, some butter, six over-ripe bananas, some fresh flour tortillas and some more bungee cords. The words 'fresh' and 'small' kept figuring in our purchases. These items filled Gary's tramping pack. He strapped them tightly to the back of the snow machine along with the survival kit.

We decided we should head back. It was ten to four.

As we headed out of St Mary's, the few added grocery items strapped on behind made the snow machine noticeably heavier. In order to manoeuvre the narrow winding trails with any agility, Gary was now required to travel at speeds closer to 30–45 mph. I knew there was no alternative. I closed my eyes, and tried not to look down at the hard ice that whizzed past my boots.

It was much warmer though, and pleasantly so. The coldness and freezing were not an issue. I was very thankful for that.

We were now roaring straight up ridges with no knowledge of the drops, or potential cliffs beyond. At our now higher speeds I knew that split-second decisions on which direction we should be going were necessary at the apex of each ridge. It was a case of total concentration by Gary and fervent prayer by me.

I thudded him on the shoulder and he shrugged. 'GO SLOWER!' I yelled. He immediately obliged, but I could feel the strain on the machine as it bit into the hills and tried to mount the snowy ridges.

The next moment I heard Gary actually swear. Then I saw a bush immediately ahead. Crash! We were both flung into the snow. The snow machine was lying on top of us. Gary lay with his head facing me. His eyes were closed. My first thought was, Is he unconscious? How can I move him or the machine? How on earth will I get out of here? There were stains of deep red in the snow.

'Gary, Gary, sweetheart! Are you okay?' His eyes flicked open. He grinned. 'Just doing a check of my body,' he announced. 'Everything's working. You?'

Amazingly I could move my legs, even though they were under the machine. The snow was so soft I could wriggle out from underneath.

'Yeah, I'm fine.' We both stood up. The machine was on its side. I pointed to the large red stain in the snow. The deep maroon colour looked like blood. It looked like we had had a major accident.

'What's that?'

'Only oil, we're fine.'

With both of us straining to lift it, we were eventually able to turn the sno-go back upright. The pack had remained strapped on.

Gary started the machine again. No problems. He pulled out twigs from the runners. It was hard to believe we were fine, but we were. But where *were* we?

Gary had been following the trail of snow machines as we had done previously, but the many ski tracks we started with had now singled down to only one.

We did a stocktake. There had been no backbreaking washboard track. We could see ahead the large ridge that marked the river turnoff to Pilot Station. We were definitely heading in the right direction, but not on the main trail that we had travelled on. With the afternoon cooling down, we decided to press on.

Five minutes later we came to a steep ridge. It was almost vertical. Unable to rise to this challenge, the machine ploughed into it and ground to a stop. We were stuck. Heavy duty stuck. I attempted to get off, a mammoth task fighting against gravity. When I eventually stepped from the bike I stepped waist deep into very soft snow. This was definitely not good. Gary attempted to rev the bike back up and out. With each rev it became buried more deeply.

Suddenly, without warning, two snow machines pulled up behind us. It was a young Yup'ik couple, each on a snow machine. He was a big man.

'*Waqaa*, we follow your trail,' he said.

'*Waqaa.* This trail goes to Pilot Station?' Gary asked. The man grinned and nodded, pointing to some distant horizon with his gloved hand.

'Main trail over there.'

Gary and this stranger eventually lifted the bike out. They had to remove the pack to do so. Time was moving on. There was now a chill in the air. Eventually they got the snow machine up the ridge. Then the man returned to his bike and took a different approach. He got stuck too. Gary helped him out.

His girlfriend, still sitting on her bike and watching it all, smiled at us. Then without a word, she revved her bike up to about 100 mph and sailed straight between both snow machines. She sailed straight up and over the ridge. She waited for us up on the other side. I tried not to smile. Women.

We told the couple to go on ahead, we'd follow. I was thankful they were with us.

Well, so much for that. Within five minutes they had disappeared, travelling at their usual frenetic speeds. So Gary just followed their tracks. We followed on and on. Eventually we saw their tracks separate then turn. They came heading back towards us. We all stopped.

'Those tracks trapper's trail. We go back to river,' the man explained. We turned too. I remembered a trail much further back I had seen going over a steep ridge. I did not want to go that way, but it appeared that that was the only way to go.

By this time we had been on the trail an hour and still the Pilot Station ridge lay well ahead. I was getting more and more worried. The afternoon was now drawing into cold. I made a mental note of the contents of our pack. Plenty there to eat. I had learned from *Tisha* that you could eat raw potatoes.

We hit another slough, but this one was filled with yellow ice. Danger. Gary sped up. We had no choice. Apparently a snow machine can 'float' over water provided there is hard ice on each side, and if you travel fast enough.

Suddenly up ahead, there was our male friend. Stopped. I saw him throw his fan belt into the bushes. 'What's up?'

'Broken fanbelt. Girlfriend ahead.' He was as pleased to see us as we had originally been pleased to see him.

'I have a spare,' said Gary. 'Want to see if it fits?'

'*Quyana*. Thanks.' He smiled. 'Girlfriend has spare wrapped round windscreen.' Spare fan belts, rather like spare tyres, were essential on such journeys. Breaking down out here could be dangerous.

Gary lifted up our engine cover to get the spare fanbelt for him, and noticed that our oil sump had lost its lid. Our friend loaned us a rubber band, and we fashioned an oil cover from a plastic bag. Gary secured it with the rubber band over the oil sump.

Gary and the man talked about the track. He reassured Gary. '*Ii-i*, that steep hill takes you through woods and back by airport.' We were apparently on a circular route from Pilot Station to St Mary's. I was very anxious about the vertical climb ahead.

'Isn't there any other way of getting there along the river?'

The man shook his head. 'Too far back, get cold now.' Deep shadows were forming on the ice. He knew I wasn't happy. 'I stay ahead,' he offered. He was so easily capable of zooming off.

Together we sped back along the large patches of that dreadful brown ice awash with surface water. We then turned and shot straight up a steep ridge. It immediately turned into a narrow wooded track that climbed and climbed and climbed.

Our new friend was true to his word. He stayed close by, turning and checking all the way. Suddenly we came out of the trees and I could recognise the snow plateau of my snow machining trials. I could see Pilot Station over the hill. The weather had cleared. In moments we would be home. What a feeling of deep relief. Our friend sped off.

On our arrival Gary immediately rang James. It was now 6 pm. James was very pleased we'd rung as he was starting to wonder whether he should summon help. Gary relayed our saga.

'Yeah, done that myself,' he told Gary. 'Bit earlier in the day, though.'

As I put the groceries away I could not believe that we had travelled all that way and exposed ourselves to such risk, for such small things.

A small bag of potatoes would never appear the same to me again.

Chapter 40

One January Day

Our wedding ceremony was a traditional Maori Anglican service. It was officiated by Lem, the Maori priest. We followed Maori protocol. As tangata whenua – representing Maori from the Otago land – Mona called us into the church. As manuhiri – representing the visitors – Paratai made the responding call. The call and response guided our small bridal party forward. The wind blew, lifting and carrying these plaintive chants, these karanga, out across the paddocks where the sheep grazed in the midsummer sun.

With me clutching my father's arm, our small party walked onto the grassy apron stretch that led up to the church. A lone Scottish bagpipe player standing under a tree there picked up the call.

The wedding guests had begun by standing outside behind Mona as she began her karanga. When the bagpipes started they all moved inside. The church was quiet except for the shuffling of feet and the odd cough.

John the choirmaster faced the small choir of 20 who were standing at the ready at the right of the altar. He was holding his baton aloft and trying to quell his rising panic. A conversation with Lem had thrown him into unusual turmoil.

'We are going to be doing this song as well,' Lem had announced, passing him several hastily photocopied sheets of choir music.

'How Great Thou Art?' John looked at Lem.

Lem smiled reassuringly. 'Ae, in English and in Maori.'

The choir, resplendent in their uniform of soft green shirts and black skirts, had had a quick practice, singing their way through this new sheet music, while they were waiting out the back of the church. One of the choir members was Maori. She had given everyone the correct pronunciation. There had been time for only three or four run-throughs, as they could hear the karanga starting out the front. They had to file quickly through the narrow doorway that led out onto the altar.

John smiled nervously. He tapped the stand. Then he nodded at the choir in a perfunctory and commanding way, instilling a confidence he didn't yet feel. He turned to look at the door. He had been a school principal once. He could pull this off.

Inside was quiet with expectancy. 'Your one chance to bolt,' whispered Gary's best man Robert. Gary grinned at him nervously. Some humour helped.

I had to stop at the door and check the deep sobs that had welled up inside me with the emotion of it all. The karanga had deeply affected me. The pipes were so moving; their tonal quality seemed to reverberate in my bones.

My father patted my arm. He produced a comb and a large handkerchief from his top pocket. He gently combed my fringe into some kind of order. I dabbed my eyes.

Ella led us into the church. She looked stunning. Her knee length fitted green dress was so dark it was almost black. She had draped a gold stole around her shoulders.

Jenny gave me a quick kiss and followed Ella. Dad gently led me forward. My long gold coat flowed out behind me in the dimly lit church. My bouquet was huge and the long ferns tipped the floor. As we entered the tiny church I could see Gary looking for me. He smiled so reassuringly and lovingly at me that my eyes welled up again. Robert stood alongside him, grinning.

The large, circular, stained window above appeared to illuminate the entire room in colourful fingers of magical light. I managed a wavering smile back at Gary. I walked slowly down the aisle towards him and our new life together.

The ceremony was mostly in Maori. Every time John played the organ he had to disappear through a small door. He would then reappear through a different door next to the organ. He reminded me of a small figurine on a German cuckoo clock, coming and going.

At one point Lem made an announcement.

'This is for Gary's mother in Illinois. We will now sing "How Great Thou Art".' That was a surprise to me, but very fitting. I squeezed Gary's hand. He looked at me with tears in his eyes.

The choir sang the hymn so beautifully. They even attempted the words in Maori. The congregation, in appreciation of that gesture, swelled the volume, and John played the entire hymn again, with everyone joining in. It helped that there were quite a few musical people in the crowd.

Lem declared us married.

'Help me, this is very heavy,' I whispered to Gary as we turned to face everyone.

'Whoa,' he muttered as he got a feel for the weight of the huge bouquet I was holding. His duties as my husband had begun.

Merv and Evelyn had a special seat in the front row. Merv had been preoccupied with capturing the ceremony on his equipment. He smiled up at us. He was pleased with the sound quality.

As we faced the congregation as husband and wife, the choir sang 'The Irish Blessing' to us. The church bell tolled its celebration, and the piper lilted 'Flower of Scotland' to the wind. We walked back down the aisle together, periodically stopping to greet our friends.

Guests and visitors all tumbled out into the wind, chatting animatedly and snapping photos.

'What a wonderful wedding,' seemed to be the consensus.

'So moving.'

Lem told me later it had ranked as one of his top favourite weddings of all time.

'Haere mai, haere mai,' called Paratai, welcoming everyone and guiding them into the little country hall that sat alongside the church. It was warm, cosy and out of the wind in there.

Inside the hall there was a delicious smell of home baking. Large urns of tea could be seen through the little counter. On a trestle table, rows of cups, bowls of white sugar, instant coffee and jugs of milk were all laid out. There were also plates and plates of home baking, club sandwiches, pikelets, cream cakes, sponges and hot savouries.

My idea had been to feed those who were not coming back to the formal reception. A cup of tea and sandwich, before driving back home. The choir was there, the piper and his family, work colleagues, local principals, my neighbours and my family.

Paratai said later, 'Sorry darling, I don't think I was supposed to invite everyone in there. It was lovely though, wasn't it?' It was.

The local countrywomen, looking slightly askance at the number and mixture of people in this little church hall, poured the tea and smiled. They'd been expecting about 30. However, having been through lambing, shearing and other unpredictable disasters, they had no trouble handling the 50 or so extra people.

In typical country style, there was plenty of food there. The scones, club sandwiches and cream cakes were all washed down with gallons of tea. In the end the women pouring the tea also came out and just joined in as well. It was a lively time. Celebratory. Loud chatter and the clinking of crockery added percussion to the late summer afternoon.

The piper chatted with Ella. The Maori priest was in deep conversation with a local sheep farmer. My primary school teacher and Mona were chatting. The local mayor, who had lent us his gold car for the day, had cornered Jenny. John was chatting with my mother about the singing, and Paratai was busy steering my father around the room.

Eventually it was time for those coming to the wedding reception to head off. Gary and I went back along the road for some wedding pics. Jenny and Ella joined us in some more photos in the homestead garden.

By the time we got to the reception everyone was very comfortable in each other's company. The buzzing atmosphere proved that friendships had been made. The wedding breakfast was set out in the formal dining room of the manor. It was buffet and included vegetarian dishes. There was a seafood platter, large ham, rolled stuffed pork, chicken, ostrich and plenty of wine.

Along with the booking of the entire manor for the afternoon, we had also booked out the three bedrooms for the wedding party that night. That had been my parents' wedding present to us.

Paratai's cake was on a special stand at the entrance to the homestead. It had been decorated with flora from out of the large gardens where the reception was being held. It looked fittingly spectacular, standing in pride of place by the front door.

Our wedding day was a golden one. We ate and toasted and introduced everyone to each other as part of the reception. After our wedding breakfast Gary stood and performed a mihi, reciting his whakapapa – his lineage and background – to me in Maori. It was an emotional surprise and so perfect for our special occasion.

Paratai had schooled him for hours down at the beach at Kotahitanga. Armed with a long stick that she used to flick seaweed and hunt for things in the sand, she would give Gary another line to practise.

'No Villa Grove ahau.' I come from Villa Grove.

Gary would then repeat the strange language to the thrashing waves. 'No Villa Grove, um.'

Paratai would listen to it, repeat it, and then walk away.

Then Gary would say it over again, this time trying to elongate the vowel in 'No', but mispronouncing 'ahau' so it sounded like he was talking about a garden tool. '*No* Villa Grove a "hoe",' he would say. Again and again he tried, till at last he got it. 'No Villa Grove ahau.'

When they got to naming his mountain, Paratai couldn't believe he had no mountain to name.

'No mountain where you come from?' she asked again.

'No ma'am, none.' Gary told her. 'It's flat corn field country as far as the eye can see.'

At the end of the reception Gary had organised for us to dance 'The Tennessee Waltz'. After we had danced for a while, Dad cut in and took over. Gary danced with Jenny and then with Ella. Everyone clapped in delight.

The photographer took a special photo of us with our wedding cake.

'Oh, wow!' said Gary, reading the inscriptions on the miniature computer screens that I'd placed on top of the cake. 'Perfect, Sunshine.'

On one screen the inscription read *'Emzel: Kia Ora from New Zealand'*; and on the other screen *'Kotzman: Taikuu from Kotzebue'*.

Everyone loved it.

Gary and I honeymooned in Lake Te Anau at Mona's holiday house. Bel came with us. It was a peaceful interlude. We had placed a book at the reception for everyone to sign. On our honeymoon we read the entries. In his beautiful handwriting Dad had written: 'One of a handful of memorable days in our lifetime. May you always remember this day with the same nostalgia all your lives, Dad and Mum.'

Ella wrote, 'To the Newly Weds, May you cherish this day always and enjoy each other for the rest of your lives. All my love Mum and new Step Dad, your daughter Ella xxxx. Bel sends her love too.'

After this late summer holiday social whirlwind and quiet honeymoon, I would have to return to school. The New Zealand school year started in early February. I would also need to settle down for my final year of study. A new year of work, now as a married woman.

Chapter 41

End of Year Activities

One morning in late April I was alerted by the melting snow. Large thuds like birds hitting the windows had me running to look outside. Huge lumps of snow and icicles were melting from our roof and hitting the steps. Children had been warned to stay away from the walls of the school buildings at this dangerous time of year. The icicles were like spears dropping from a great height. Eskimo children took snow warnings seriously. There had been no accidents.

The foot tracks to our house had become slushy and muddy. Finally I could walk to the post office with my nose remaining at room temperature. Everyone seemed amused to hear me still arriving in my ice cleats. Treacherous sheets of ice still hid beneath the surface. I had watched the locals moving stealthily and silently in their *mukluks*, thinking I needed more practice. I then discovered the reason why the grey fur-lined boots that I purchased in Anchorage had been on special. The inverted treads filled with snow and became slick. Until I discovered this was the reason, I found myself falling over constantly.

I baked a birthday cake for one of the elders, and we took it to Eskimo dancing to celebrate his birthday with him there. Lack of dental care and the expense of dentures meant that many of the elders had various teeth missing. The toothless 75-year-old pulled on the flannel shirt and fluorescent pink lei we had given him and looked as pleased as a five-year-old with a birthday toy.

The cake was cut and shared around. The elders came over to us, nodding their heads slowly and respectfully as a polite gesture of deference, and smiling and shaking our hands. They didn't sit and give a quick nod at us, as they had at our first meetings.

At a recent potlatch with St Mary's village, Gary and I had been asked to join in the dancing. Later our elders introduced us to the elders of St Mary's. Gary was encouraged to show them the haka. He had learnt the haka during a weekend wananga, an educational forum I had held for Maori students in Otago. He had terrified locals earlier in the school year before my arrival by presenting a rendition of this Maori warrior dance.

Gary got up with the geography teacher. He had been warned that he was going to be asked to perform a haka, and the two had been practising. They lifted the roof with a couple of lines of 'Ka mate, ka mate'. To wild glee from the audience, the St Mary's chief got up and faced off with Gary during the haka. He playfully mimicked Gary's actions. There was uproarious laughter and loud clapping from the animated large crowd. It was then my turn.

I sang a Maori waiata-ringa, a song with actions. I was accompanied by one of the older elementary girls, Suzie, who had asked to learn the song when I performed it for her class.

'This song describes the snow falling on the mountains in the South Island of New Zealand, where I was born.' I spoke loud and slow. I also showed the action with my hands so that they could see it. Twiddling my fingers in a downward motion, I made a mountain peak. Suzie translated my words into Yup'ik, showing the same action. We had practised together. We wanted everyone to understand what he or she was about to see.

'The snow melts down the mountain sides like tears,' I continued, rippling my fingers in a downward movement from my eyes. I waited for Suzie to speak and repeat the action. 'It flows into the rivers,' a sideways long movement. 'It's bringing strength and growth to the earth there.' My fists opened, lifting my hands up and over in an action like growth. Suzie spoke and repeated the action perfectly. She looked at me. I nodded.

We began to sing, '*Tau ana hukarere, ki ruka Aoraki . . .*' The haunting melody made an impact. There was pure silence at the strange but familiar-sounding words.

As the audience watched our hands tell the story, I noticed some of the younger children copying. We turned our bodies in unison, stamping the floor with our socks to give the rhythm. Our voices filled the hushed space, just as theirs had done before us.

Our item had been different from anything they had ever witnessed before, yet strangely the same. Everyone talked about it for days afterwards.

The landscape now underwent dramatic changes by the day. I was amazed to see Gary's walking track to school change so quickly. The week before it had been in deep snow, but now like warmed invisible ink the track gradually appeared as brown mud.

Long trickles of water ran downhill to the road. The snow became translucent and dribbled, then trickled away. The sound of many little brooks ran through the quiet countryside.

Gumboots, rather than snow boots were pulled out, and the porch area became filthy with mud imprints. These didn't magically melt away as the snow had done for so long.

In two weeks winter had ended, we had had spring and were now experiencing summer. Around the village there was still much snow tucked deep into the valleys and spread across the hills. The brown tundra was now exposed. The snow machines had finally been silenced. Four-wheelers were now back on the track. They were throwing up sheets of dust again.

As well, all that had lain beneath that Persil-white snow was now rudely exposed. There was litter everywhere. Rough piles of long planks of timber and large machine parts lay abandoned where they had been used. An old red wheelbarrow, tyres, very many squashed soda cans and large broken sections of discarded gib-board were strewn everywhere. Rusted bands of steel that secured the hundreds of connexes filled with equipment for the new school lay in discarded piles. Looking at the many rusty traps there, I was grateful I never tripped and fell deeply into that snow-covered debris.

'Look, honey.' Gary called me to the front porch one morning. 'Watch the river.' The ice appeared to be moving on the surface of the mighty Yukon River. We lined it up with a landmark.

'Wow, it sure is moving,' I answered, grabbing the binoculars off the windowsill.

'Yeah, and fast.'

The next day I could see reflections of clouds in the river. It appeared as if it had never been frozen. Such a magical trick, a deft transformation from frozen to thawed in one day. The river reminded me of someone who had suffered a long time with cataracts, snowy and frosted vision, then suddenly on one clear May day had received laser surgery from the piercing sunshine. Its vision was now pure and transparent. The river could see again.

Large ice biscuits approximately four metres square passed swiftly down the river. They would float on out to the Bering Sea. Little runabouts could now be seen puttering along amongst it all. It was a spectacular phenomenon.

Sunlight lit our days from 6 am to midnight. The temperature was creeping up to 70 degrees by 9:30 in the morning, but there was no chance of a refreshing shower.

'Water's off again!' Gary announced one morning.

'Oh no,' I grumbled. 'I meant to do the washing this morning.'

This time it would be off for three days. The city was digging up the pipelines. They would eventually discover the leak that had robbed us of so much water over winter.

Daylight felt continuous now, mainly because the sun was well up when we woke and was still shining brightly when it was bedtime, around ten or eleven at night. It was difficult to adjust to. My internal sleeping clock appeared to be tuned to darkness. In Balclutha, I had put up dark curtains to block out the long twilight hours of early summer. But really there was no comparison; the sun was still shining here at midnight.

I came to understand the problem the students had after a long summer of midnight sun here. In the new school year they would constantly fall asleep in class.

Gary started bossing me just like a good parent. 'It's bedtime, honey,' he would say at about 9 pm. He knew with all my muttering about it still being daylight that it would take me an hour or so to finally get to bed. But it worked. This way I didn't need to catch up on sleep till noon the following day.

Huge shock and happy surprise, I passed all of the Praxis papers. And passed quite well. I was very proud of myself. Gary's pride was tempered with relief.

Gary and I were leaving. We had been offered jobs as principal and first grade teacher at a very respected village in the South West of Alaska. We were now packing, again. The packing, labelling, fretting and worrying if the loads would reach their destinations occupied most of my days and nights.

During the last week of school both graduation and the prom were scheduled. The graduation was held the night before the prom. There was only one student eligible to graduate. This girl had had her baby the week before. Some of her expected assignments were still not passed in. The staff organising the evening's function were unsure what to do. Would there be a graduation ceremony or not? Gary rang home.

'Has Gabrielle completed her assignments?'

Her mom did not know. 'She in Bethel for baby check-up.'

There was mighty relief when Gabrielle wandered in early afternoon with all her assignments completed.

I was so excited to be going to my very first prom. I decided I would even paint my fingernails for the occasion.

'Wow, honey,' Gary breathed at this strange new woman standing before him, 'You look beautiful.' I had dressed in my green wedding dress finery.

'You look handsome yourself,' I said, blushing under his stare. He wore his wedding shirt and tie, black suit jacket and pants.

Gary borrowed the school pickup to drive me to the school. The humour of our Alaskan predicament hit us. First the truck was quite dirty and dusty. There had been no point in cleaning it. Sitting parked out the front of our place it would quickly be covered again in very fine silt dust. 'Just imagine it waxed and polished to a red mirror magic,' said Gary with a chuckle.

'Well,' I grinned. 'Then you need to imagine *me* wearing my gold dancing shoes, just like Cinderella.' I had them in a plastic bag under my arm. On my feet were my trusty gumboots.

'You look cute, honey,' Gary said, smiling lovingly at me.

True love, that, I thought privately.

Next Gary couldn't open the truck door for me. He had to clamber in across the bench seat ahead of me through the passenger's door. The driver's door had been taped up with duct tape, after a recent 'accident'.

We arrived at the school in almost one whole minute. We went into Gary's office where I changed into my magic golden slippers. Arm in arm we picked our way across the planked and filthy walkway between buildings. I imagined that we looked as if we had stepped out of the pages of a prince and princess book. I could almost hear the universal in-take of breath.

In the middle of my reverie I was rather startled to see some of the kids gawking at us dressed in their usual gear, jeans and running shoes. My greatest surprise, however, was yet to come. My husband disappeared into a classroom and reappeared flourishing a rose. A real red rose. He pinned it onto my dress and arm in arm again we glided into the school's gymnasium.

There I received my second stunning surprise of the evening. I knew the room had been painstakingly prepared for the previous night's graduation ceremony. Long pink sheets of paper had been hung from roof height around the walls. They were stapled down with bunches of pink and white balloons. Tables and candles had been added for the prom night. They too had all been decorated in a pink and white theme.

However the room was in total darkness. It was like walking into a photographer's dark room. Gary seemed not at all surprised at the pitch-blackness. He had been to other dances.

'There's Annette sitting over there,' Gary said.

'Where?' I couldn't see anything. I wondered if I had suddenly become blind with detached retinas, like I'd seen on the Discovery Channel that afternoon.

Gary led me over to Annette and once I was safely sitting, things started to appear through the gloom. A disco rig was set up on a makeshift stage. A 'blue light' shone out onto the floor, where pink and white balloons were carefully scattered. I remained incredulous. Was this how it would be, in the *dark*!

'Kids like to think it's night,' Annette explained. Although it was already 9 pm, the sun was still shining brightly outside, just like midday. 'They are inherently shy,' she patted my hand. 'They'll only get up and dance in the dark.' That room was like any midnight night-club I had ever been in.

Gary asked me to dance. We loved to dance in old style. We would impress any one who could see movement in the dark. We swirled around, having great fun. From then on, even though all the music was rap music, I danced and danced and danced. I got to dance with the single male teachers. Gary got to dance with the females. Then we showed off our inimitable style together. I loved it all.

We staggered out to bright sunshine at 11 pm. I had to put my gumboots back on. We would walk home, as the truck had been dispatched for more urgent business elsewhere. I clutched my red rose with an idiotic grin of a totally pleasurable evening. What a night!

All the faculty were returning to the Lower 48 for their summer vacations. They would be back late August, in autumn. There was a constant stream of visitors to the house. Locals, teachers and even some of the students all came to say goodbye in their own personal and touching ways. We promised to stay in touch and shared addresses.

Gary and I would be flying straight to our new school district. I had to miss my own graduation in New Zealand – I could not leave this country because of immigration restrictions. I still had not heard from the US Department of Homeland Security. Our new superintendent had not been at all concerned that I did not yet have a social security number essential for employment.

One week after the prom and even in the intense heat of the sun, the rose still looked in its prime. I had placed it on the shelf in the bedroom and sniffed its fresh rose fragrance each day. On our last night Gary had kissed me. Lovingly he said, 'Maybe it's a special hybrid Alaskan rose, honey, just like you.'

Chapter 42
Alaska Calls

After the honeymoon I had settled down to a new year of work. Gary had visited the local kohanga reo, the infant school where all lessons were given in Maori, several times. He had written a paper on the early childhood immersion program for speakers of Maori. He sent it off to the Alaskan Department of Education to be assessed. The credit he would receive for completing this paper would keep his Alaskan administrator's certification current. Soon after his arrival he had sent his papers to the New Zealand Qualifications Authority (NZQA) for assessment to teach in New Zealand.

Gary received his credentials back, translated into a provisional practising certificate by the NZQA. It was completed quite quickly. He had recently started talking about teaching again.

'I got a call from Milton High School,' he told me excitedly one day late in March. 'I'm doing some casual teaching there tomorrow.' Milton had been one of the local schools he had visited to leave his name as a reliever.

Gary couldn't wait to report his experience at the end of the first day. 'You know honey, I had to fill in notebooks for each class,' he reported. 'And everyone stopped at 10:30 for a cup of tea!' There was that refueling business again that had so intrigued him.

Other days he came with me to the country schools. 'Just for the ride, honey.' Gary was very impressed with the resource teacher model. He thought it would be excellent in Alaskan schools. He thought teachers there would greatly welcome that level of support.

One day he saw a job advertised as a professor at Dunedin University in the teacher preparation programme there. It was in the Education Department. I drove him through to the interview in Dunedin.

'I think I did okay,' he said after the interview. 'They were quite interested in my experience.' We chatted happily on the drive home. Maybe he would get a job in Dunedin. That would be great.

In the end it was not to be. He was short listed but missed out. The depth of his disappointment in missing out on this job was an indicator to us both. He needed to be back in the education system again. He also wanted to be a breadwinner. It had been nearly a year since he had left Kotzebue. Gary was ready for work again.

One night in late March, Jared called Gary from Pilot Station, in bush Alaska. Jared had been Gary's deputy in Kotzebue, and they had had sporadic email contact over the past year. Jared knew Gary was having difficulty in getting work in New Zealand.

'Hey, Doc. I am resigning this position as principal in Pilot Station. I'm heading home to South Carolina with the family.' Jared's first year as a principal had been in the Lower Yukon, at Pilot Station. Jared's wife had not been well. He wanted her to get stronger. Bush living could be challenging. 'I've spoken to the superintendent about you. He is keen.'

A new school was planned for Pilot Station for the following year. There was much to be done. They needed an experienced principal. 'Doc, we need you out here,' Jared had said. I could see Gary was excited. Someone knew about him and wanted his experience. It made him feel good.

If Gary completed five more years in the Alaskan Teacher Retirement System, he could retire with a monthly stipend paid in US dollars. He would also get long-term health care. American dollar signs floated before my eyes.

'Sweetheart,' I said. 'We need to talk.'

It was yet another late night conversation. 'I really don't want to move from New Zealand,' I said, once again. I could hear the whine in my voice. 'I love my job.' I also had a great boss who had been so supportive. 'It has taken me years to finally come home to New Zealand. I can't *bear* the thought of moving again.'

Gary nodded. He knew.

'I told you you'd never have to leave New Zealand again. I would never ask you to, honey.' He looked incredibly sad. 'Sunshine, I don't want to go either. I sure don't want to leave you. I just can't see getting any work here.'

Gary had just gained New Zealand residency. We'd had to submit scrapbooks with engagement cards, newspaper announcement of our wedding, and support letters from friends. It had been a nightmare of red tape, affidavits and legal documents. Apparently marrying someone you met off the internet did not impress the New Zealand Immigration Department. Leaving again would mean Gary would jeopardise his residency.

I thought of a plan. 'I know,' I countered. 'If we look at the school calendars in both countries, we could each live in different places, but still spend our long holidays together.' I smiled sweetly, but Gary didn't look at all impressed. I tried to sound very enthusiastic. 'Even if we lived in different hemispheres, our down time would still be together.' I also knew it would mean eternally wintering in each other's places. 'Just think.' I ended in a flourish. 'We'd have little actual time apart!'

I pushed the idea of going to that distant planet of Alaska to the back of my mind. Even visiting Gary in that bleak faraway place did not appeal to me at all.

'I'm not so sure, honey,' Gary looked very doubtful.

'But how else will you get an opportunity like this?' I was warming to my topic. 'Jared has set it up for you.' It would mean Gary would not have to travel to the Alaskan April Job Fair. 'You wouldn't need to make two trips. You could just go straight there!' I was starting to get through to him.

'Yeah, that's true.' Gary said thoughtfully. 'I'm just not sure leaving you is the right thing to do.'

I finished imbuing my words with an optimism I didn't really feel. 'I am *sure* we could manage it. *We* can manage *anything*.'

Gary mulled over this idea for several days. We talked further. I was firm in my resolution. I definitely didn't want to live in Alaska. I was home. I wouldn't be budging. Anyway, Gary had promised when we married that I would never have to leave New Zealand again. I kept on reminding him.

The prospect of having a job ready and waiting won him over in the end. My positive attitude about how we could manage it and the need to make a fast decision helped.

'You can always come back at the end of the school year if it doesn't work for us.' I hugged him, feeling a bit sick that he was now actually contemplating leaving.

'All my stuff is here,' he groaned. 'More shipping.' Most of his important belongings were now in New Zealand. The prospect of thinking about what he would need to take all the way back was definitely daunting.

As the date for his departure drew ever closer, we discussed how we would manage this farewell. In a symbolic gesture, Gary decided that he wanted to leave from the Balclutha railway station. 'I'll farewell you and Bel at the place I returned to you,' he said. He would then travel by the Southerner up to Christchurch and stay overnight with my parents. 'I'll fly from Christchurch to Auckland and Seattle. From there I will fly back to Alaska.'

It was a sad journey to the Balclutha railway station for both of us.

When the day arrived, I could not really believe that we were going to be separated again. We would be back to writing daily emails as before. I wondered how we would sustain the regimen of daily writing again. The novelty of the new and undiscovered was now long lost. We knew we were going to be severely tested.

I took a photo of that departure and put it on the mantelpiece in my little flat to stare at. Gary, suitcases stacked at his feet, holding his beloved Bel in one arm, smiling sadly into the camera. We had both tried to be brave.

'Well, Sunshine, this is it.' He gave me a huge bear hug.

'Have fun,' I said lamely.

When the train arrived Gary hugged me one last time, grabbed his bags, and jumped aboard. He gave a small wave from the window. I stood alone on the platform with Bel.

The Southerner blew a long mournful whistle. With a lurch and rattle the train slowly chugged on down the line. It was taking Kotzman away from me, taking him all the way back to Alaska where he had come from.

Acknowledgements

Thanks to Ro Cambridge for her practical, warm and enthusiastic mentorship throughout the year's long journey to print and for lending her writing and design skills to this project. Also to Jeanette Cook of Cook Publishing for her inspired editing, and Chrissie Ward for her close attention to detail.

    Special thanks to Conor Quinn, First Words Writing Service, for wading through the original manuscript and giving particularly helpful advice.

www.walkingonice.co.nz